STEP-BY-STEP

Garnishing

WENDY VEALE

STEP-BY-STEP

Garnishing

WENDY VEALE

CHARTWELL
BOOKS, INC.

For my dear family and friends, and
especially Mum, Dad and Peter

A QUINTET BOOK

Published by Chartwell Books
A Division of Book Sales, Inc.
110 Enterprise Avenue
Secaucus, New Jersey 07094

ISBN 1-55521-464-9

This book was designed and produced by
Quintet Publishing Limited
6 Blundell Street
London N7 9BH

Creative Director: Peter Bridgewater
Designer: Terry Jeavons
Project Editor: Judith Simons
Editors: Sophie Hale, Beverly LeBlanc
Photographer: Ian Howes
Home Economist: Wendy Veale

Typeset in Great Britain by
Central Southern Typesetters, Eastbourne
Manufactured in Hong Kong by
Regent Publishing Services Limited
Printed in Hong Kong by Leefung-Asco Printers Limited

ACKNOWLEDGEMENTS
The author and publishers would like to extend their thanks to
Swan Housewares Ltd for generously supplying kitchen
equipment, and also Backgrounds and R & G Stevens.

CONTENTS

INTRODUCTION

The perfect garnish should make a dish look both decorative and appetizing. But not only that; a garnish is an affectionate gesture, a compliment to your guests as well as a complement to the food.

In classical French cookery the title of a dish referred simply to the ingredients of its crowning glory, or a famous city, event or person for whom it was created. (Thus 'Mozart' conjures for the gastronome subtle harmonies of artichoke hearts stuffed with celery purée, soufflé potatoes and pepper sauce.)

Those great dishes live on, but beside them has grown up a whole new concept of garnishing, a renaissance inspired by ideas and ingredients from a vast range of culinary cultures – Japanese to Mexican, from the Americas to the Middle East, Europe to the Orient – each with a tradition of respect, for both the food and its recipient.

ABOVE A delicate Choux Pastry Swan (see page 63) can be filled with a savoury butter, pâté or cream cheese to complement your selected dish.

RIGHT Nutty Pineapple Slices (see page 28) are delicious served with pork, ham and chicken dishes.

OPPOSITE Bright red Chilli Flowers (see page 33) offer a wonderful colour contrast when teamed with a delicate green Avocado Mousse (see page 87).

With people becoming more interested in all aspects of food and its preparation (an interest focussed in some part of *nouvelle cuisine*), there seems no end to the range and ingenuity of garnishes. But their role remains constant: to make food tempting, colourful, even a work of art.

It is said (and rightly) that a dish should be a feast for the eyes as well as the stomach. Never underestimate the power of the senses as the meal – so lovingly prepared – is brought to the table: all the time spent 'slaving over a hot stove' is rewarded by that sight, that smell, that taste, and, probably, that round of applause.

Let this book show you, step by step, how to turn any dish into a celebration, and any meal into an occasion.

ABOVE Tempting Smoked Salmon Cornets (see page 82) here enhance a light Smoked Trout Mousse (see page 91).

OPPOSITE A perfect 'rose' contrived from a continuous strip of tomato skin and two mint leaves (see page 41).

RIGHT A bouquet of fresh herbs – such as thyme, mint, dill and parsley – can be tied together with a chive stem to form a natural garnish to lay beside your chosen dish.

How to choose a garnish

This book will show you something of the range of possible garnishes, with serving suggestions and variations on the most popular themes. The list on pages 110 to 111 suggests what basically goes with what, but here are a few guidelines you might find useful when choosing a garnish, or creating one of your own.

Some garnishes arise from time-honoured combinations, like lemons with fish, apples with pork, sage and onions with goose and cranberries with turkey, while others stem naturally from one of the dish's components: Tarragon Chicken, for example, simply crowned with a sprig of that aromatic herb.

Still other garnishes are chosen specifically for contrast, whether in colour, texture, richness or flavour: pink prawns against the delicate green of an avocado mousse; crisp croûtons in a creamy soup; fresh salad vegetables with a smooth pâté; a slice of seasoned butter to moisten grilled fish; the sharp simplicity of a twist of lime on a venison terrine; chilled cucumber cooling a spicy curry.

Remember that a garnish is there to enhance the food, not to disguise it, and your choice of serving dish contributes to this. Elaborate patterns can distract the eye while plain colours and simple, elegant shapes will enhance your work of art and set it off to its best advantage.

On a practical note, a garnish should be simple to assemble to avoid last-minute panics over rapidly cooling food, and easy to serve (arrange those cherries and orange slices around your duck, not on top of it).

So, bearing the above in mind, and with this book, a steady hand, and a vast array of possible ingredients to inspire you, you should be able to find the perfect garnish for any dish – and even invent a few of your own.

ABOVE This tasty Chicken, Cheese and Chive Terrine (see page 98) is decorated with pepper and egg 'flowers' and coated with aspic.

BELOW A refreshing Cucumber & Cream Cheese Mousse (see page 92) is enhanced with cucumber and star fruit (carambola).

Garnishes and recipes in this book

● Amounts of ingredients are given first in US, then metric, then imperial measures; do not combine measures within a recipe.

● All teaspoons and tablespoons are measured level.

● Where no specific quantity of garnish is recommended for a particular dish, the amount is left to the cook's individual taste.

● If a recipe is suitable for freezing, this is indicated at the end of the method.

● Some standard recipes mentioned as an integral part of the ingredients (for example, Choux Paste and Béchamel Sauce) can be found on pages 108 and 109, under the heading Basic Recipes.

● A complete list of food types and their possible garnishes is also given at the end of the book (see pages 110–111).

A Lemon Pouch is an unusual method of presenting a lemon garnish.

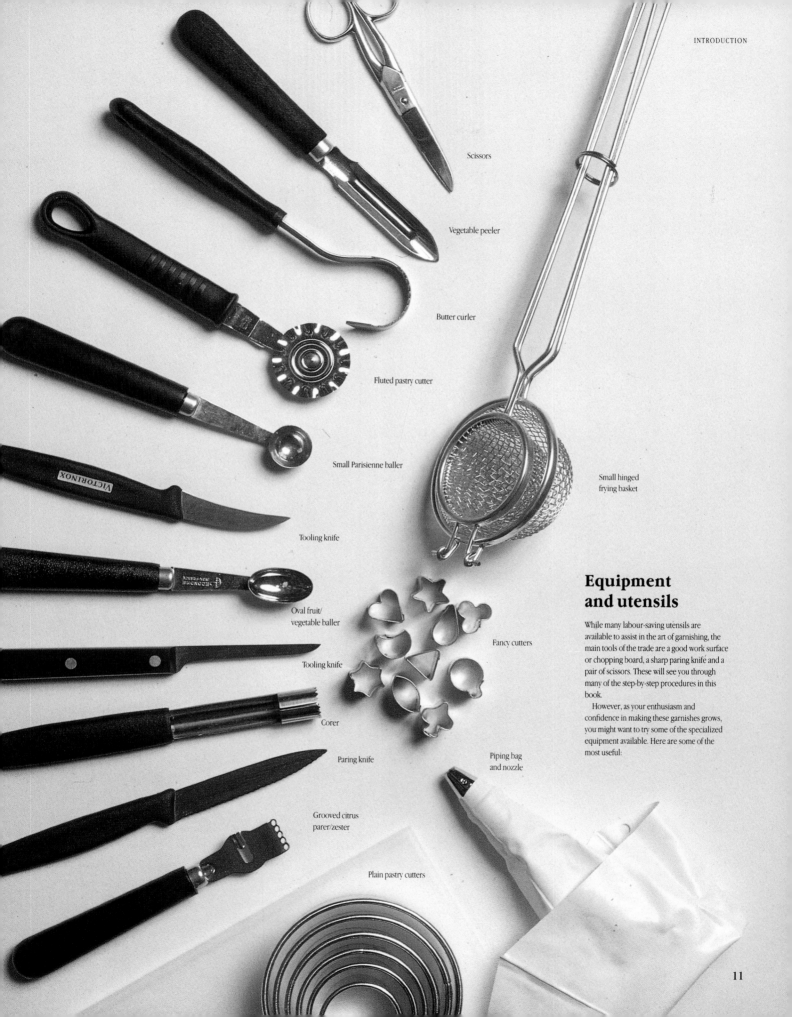

Scissors

Vegetable peeler

Butter curler

Fluted pastry cutter

Small Parisienne baller

Small hinged
frying basket

Tooling knife

Oval fruit/
vegetable baller

Fancy cutters

Tooling knife

Corer

Paring knife

Piping bag
and nozzle

Grooved citrus
parer/zester

Plain pastry cutters

Equipment and utensils

While many labour-saving utensils are available to assist in the art of garnishing, the main tools of the trade are a good work surface or chopping board, a sharp paring knife and a pair of scissors. These will see you through many of the step-by-step procedures in this book.

However, as your enthusiasm and confidence in making these garnishes grows, you might want to try some of the specialized equipment available. Here are some of the most useful:

CITRUS FRUIT GARNISHES

Lemon Half with a Knot

1

Cut a firm, unblemished lemon in half, then take a sliver off the base of the lemon so it will sit upright firmly.

3

Tie the strip into an attractive knot as shown.

VARIATION If slices with a knot are preferred, complete as above, then slice off the 'tied' part of the lemon. Repeat the process as required. Oranges and limes are also suitable for this garnish.

2

Holding a sharp paring knife or citrus cutter at a slight inward angle, peel away a ¼-in/5-mm strip of skin, almost all the way round the top edge.

Grooved Lemon Slices

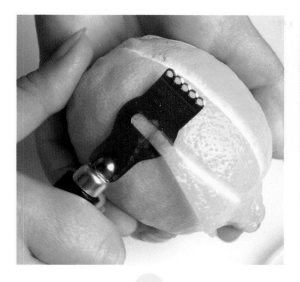

1

Using a sharp paring knife or special citrus grooving knife, make grooves along the length of the fruit from end to end.

2

Slice the lemon, approximately ¼ in/5 mm thick, but finer if they are to be twisted (see page 16).

3

The lemon slices can be pressed into some finely chopped fresh herbs to coat the flesh.

VARIATION Small oranges or limes can be used instead.

USE AS A GARNISH FOR:

PÂTÉS

MOUSSES

FISH AND SHELLFISH DISHES

VEAL AND CHICKEN DISHES

FLANS

DRINKS AND PUNCHES

Lemon Twist and Cone

USE AS A GARNISH FOR:

SHELLFISH AND FISH

MOUSSES AND FISH PÂTÉS

ORANGES AND LIMES AND FIRM-SKINNED CLEMENTINES OR MANDARINS CAN ALSO BE USED.

1

Cut a good-sized lemon into ¼ in/5-mm slices, plain or grooved, and slit the slices almost to the centre.

For a **Lemon Cone,** form a funnel, slightly overlapping one cut end with the other.

2

For a **Lemon Twist,** twist the two outer surfaces in opposite directions.

A tiny, fresh herb sprig looks attractive in the centre of the twist or cone.

Lemon Butterflies

1

Cut a good sized lemon into ¼-in/5-mm slices. Cut each slice in half, then cut the half, as if to quarter it, but without cutting right the way through to the centre.

2

Arrange the two attached triangles like a butterfly's wings and using either fine strips of chive or red pepper, make some antennae.

Twisted Lemon Fans

1

Follow the instructions for Lemon Twist, cutting three slices for each garnish needed.

Lay the cut slices one on top of the other, and twist the two outer surfaces into opposite directions.

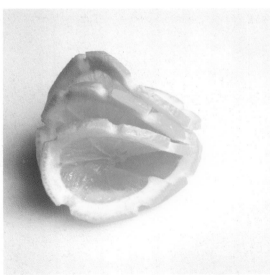

2

Separate the twists slightly to form an attractive fan and place onto a whole lemon slice.

VARIATION This looks most attractive if the lemon slices have been grooved. Small oranges or limes can also be used.

Lemon Swans

1

Cut a lemon into ¼-in/5-mm slices. Halve the slices. Cut between the peel and the pith along the length of the half slice, leaving a small section at the end connected.

2

Form the lemon peel into a loop as shown, tucking its loose end in under the attached peel.

3

Use the lemon swans singly or arrange in attractive groups.

Lemon in a Pouch

1

Cut out a round of muslin (cheesecloth), measuring approximately 8 in/20 cm across.

2

Cut a small lemon or lime in half and place one half in the centre of the muslin, cut side down. Draw up the edges to form a small pouch.

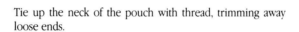

3

Tie up the neck of the pouch with thread, trimming away loose ends.

4

Using fresh herbs, as available, decoratively tuck small sprigs around the neck of the pouch.

USE AS A GARNISH FOR:

FISH AND SHELLFISH DISHES AND IN DISHES WHERE THE FRESHLY SQUEEZED JUICE IS REQUIRED

THE POUCH KEEPS FINGERS CLEAN, PREVENTS THE PIPS FROM ESCAPING AND IS SIMPLE TO PREPARE, YET LOOKS ATTRACTIVE.

Lime Basket

USE AS A GARNISH FOR:

COLD MEAT

SHELLFISH AND FISH PLATTERS

INDIVIDUAL MOUSSES AND TERRINES

BAKED WHOLE FISH DISHES

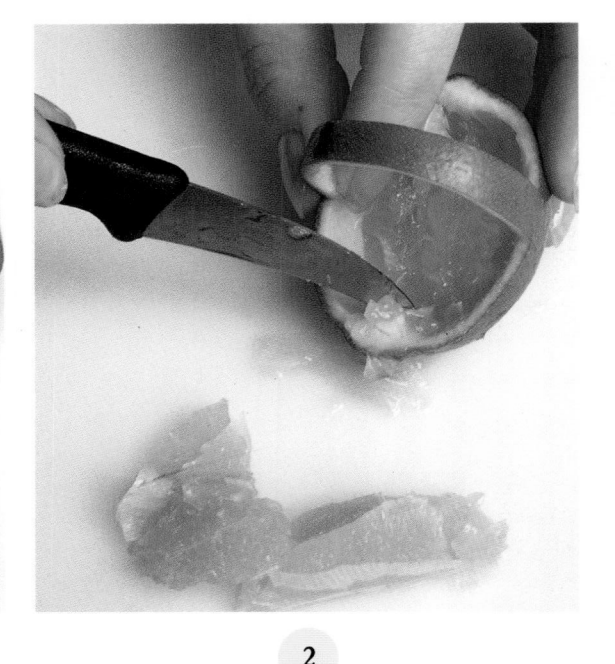

1

Select a good lime and take a fine sliver off the side of the lime so it will sit securely. Make two cuts halfway through the lime, ¼ in/5 mm apart, just either side of the centre; this will form the handle. Slice across the middle to meet the first horizontal cuts. Remove the wedge of lime. Repeat on the other side.

2

Carefully cut away the semi-circle of flesh from under the handle and scoop out all the flesh in the base of the basket.

3

Fill the miniature basket with tiny sprigs of herbs or edible greenery, small Spring Onion (Scallion) Curls (see page 39) or Chilli Flowers (see page 33).

VARIATION The basket can also be made from lemons and oranges, but these look better on larger platters.

| Orange Segments | Orange Jelly Wedges |

1

1

Using a sharp knife, take a slice off the top and base of the fruit to reveal the fruit pulp.

Cutting downwards, just inside the skin, take away the peel and white pith.

Halve an orange and scoop out the flesh.

In a small bowl, sprinkle 1 tbsp/15 ml/1 tbsp powdered gelatine over 3 tbsp/45 ml/3 tbsp water. Place over a pan of simmering water and heat gently until dissolved.

Meanwhile, gently melt scant 1 cup/200 g/7 oz redcurrant jelly in another saucepan. Stir in the dissolved gelatine.

2

2

To remove each segment, cut into the fruit, alongside the membranes of the segment. Twist the knife under and around the other side of the segment, which will then cleanly lift out. Repeat all the way round the fruit.

Stand each orange shell in a glass or cup to hold it firm. Pour the jelly into the fruit halves and refrigerate until set.

Cut into wedges for garnishing.

NOTE Any juice remaining in the fruit's membrane can be squeezed out and added to a sauce or gravy.

VARIATION This method is also applicable to lemons, grapefruits and limes. Try to select fruit without pips.

VARIATION Replace the redcurrant jelly with mint jelly and set it in lemon shells. This amount will fill two to three lemons.

ORANGE
SEGMENTS
———

USE AS A GARNISH FOR:

PÂTÉS AND MOUSSES

FISH, POULTRY AND GAME DISHES

SALADS AND COLD MEAT PLATTERS

ORANGE
JELLY WEDGES
———

USE AS A GARNISH FOR:

HOT OR COLD MEATS, GAME AND POULTRY – PARTICULARLY LAMB, DUCK AND TURKEY DISHES

Orange Julienne

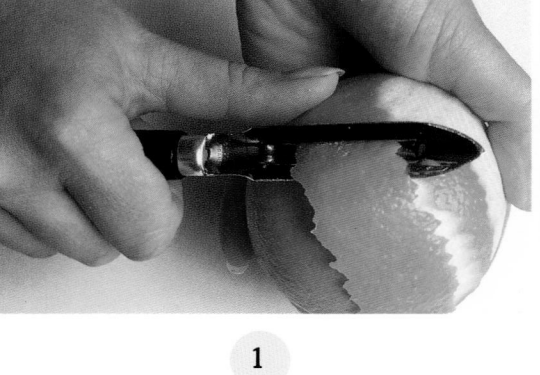

1

Using a vegetable peeler or sharp paring knife, cut the peel thinly from the fruit.

2

Using the point of the knife, scrape away any bitter white pith.

3

Trim the strips into neat lengths and then cut the peel into matchstick-wide strips.

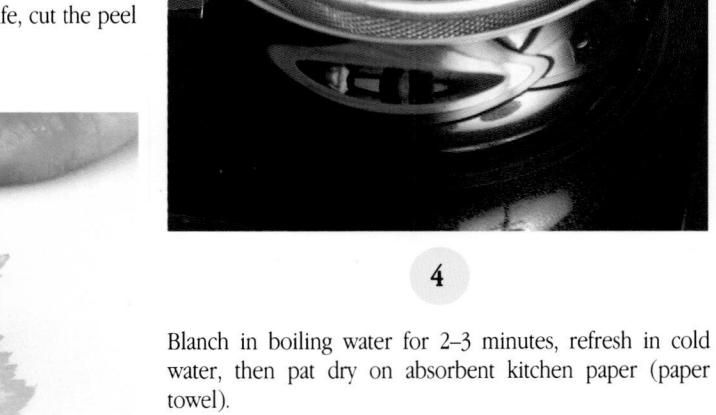

4

Blanch in boiling water for 2–3 minutes, refresh in cold water, then pat dry on absorbent kitchen paper (paper towel).

VARIATION Julienne strips can also be made from grapefruit, lemons, limes, or any other firm-skinned citrus fruit.

OTHER FRUIT GARNISHES

Apple Peony

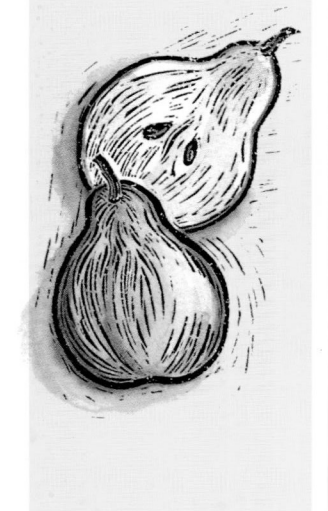

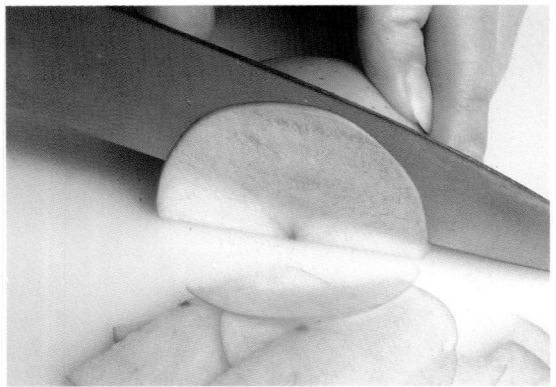

1

Have ready a bowl of well salted water with a little lemon juice added.

Cut an eating apple in half lengthwise. Lay it cut side down. With a sharp knife, cut the apple from stalk to stem in paper thin slices.

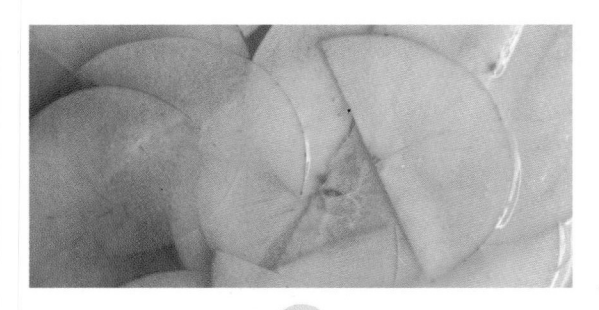

2

Drop the slices into the prepared bowl of water. Leave for half an hour. The salt will make the apple pliable, and the lemon juice will prevent discoloration.

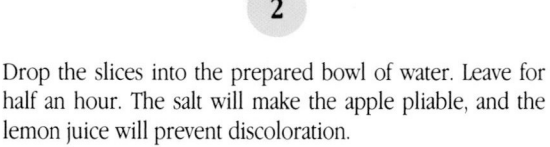

3

Take one small apple slice and roll it up to form the centre bud. Place the apple bud, skin side down.

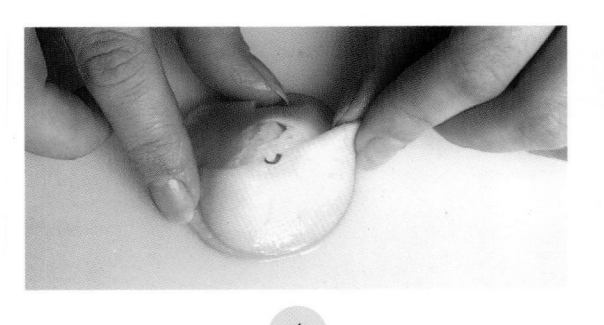

4

Arrange the remaining slices, skin side down and overlapping slightly, around the bud.

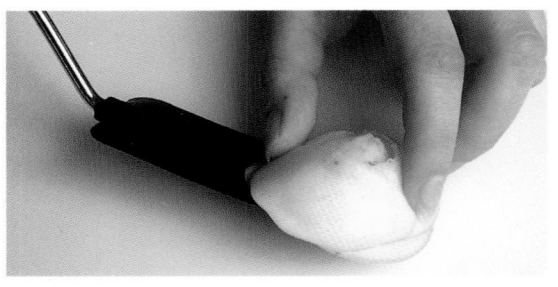

5

Use a palette knife or fish slice to turn the apple garnish the right way up and lift it into position.

VARIATION The peony can also be made from white radish (mooli or daikon), orange or lemon slices and tomatoes.

Kiwi Fans

1

Select firm, small kiwi fruits. Using a sharp paring knife, peel off the skin.

2

Cut the kiwi in half, lengthwise, and then again into quarters.

3

Cut five or six slices along the length of the kiwi as shown, stopping just short of the end.

4

With the point of the knife, carefully ease the slices open, and fan them out.

5

A small decorative chive 'bow', or a fresh herb sprig, or a small slice of strawberry can add a final touch.

Melon 'Grapes'

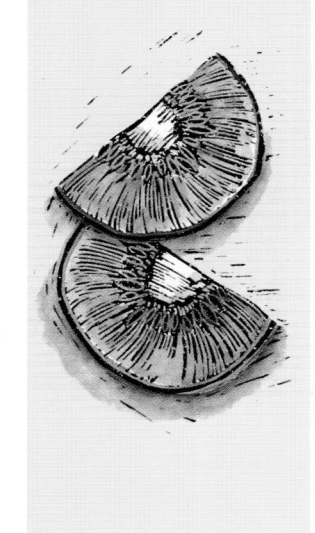

1

Any variety of ripe melon can be used to make this miniature bunch of grapes. Cut the melon in half and scoop out the seeds.

3

Arrange the balls on the serving plate, in a triangular shape, with two small coriander or flat parsley leaves at the top to represent the vine leaves, and a piece of chive stem for the stalk.

2

Using the smallest Parisienne cutter (melon baller), scoop out six balls for each garnish.

4

More melon balls can be built up to form a larger bunch of grapes, 20 to 30, say, to garnish meat, fish and cheese platters.

VARIATION Peeled cucumber can also be used. Butter balls (see page 73) also look attractive served like this.

Poached Pears

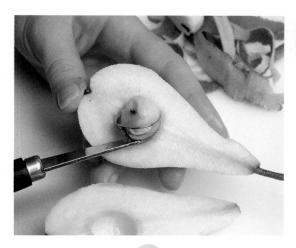

1

3

Select small, firm, but ripe pears. Peel the fruit. Have ready a bowl of water with a little lemon juice added to prevent discoloration.

Cut each pear in half lengthwise and then, with a teaspoon or Parisienne cutter (melon baller), scoop out the core to form a small cavity.

Cut a fine slice off the base of the pear so it will sit upright.

Fill the cavity with either chopped nuts and dried fruits, or a savoury butter (see page 72) and fresh herbs.

VARIATION Apples can be poached and filled in the same way. They should be peeled first, and a slice cut off top and bottom, leaving approximately two-thirds of the apple. Then, using a small, sharp knife or corer, the core can be scooped out to form a cavity.

2

Prepare a light sugar syrup by dissolving ½ cup/125 g/4 oz sugar in 1¼ cups/300 ml/½ pt water and 1 tbsp/15 ml/1 tbsp lemon juice over a low heat, then boiling for 2–3 minutes. Add the pears and gently simmer until they have softened slightly. This will take 10–15 minutes, depending upon the ripeness of the fruit.

Drain the fruit on absorbent kitchen paper (paper towel) and either keep warm or allow to cool before using.

Nutty Pineapple Slices

1

Select a small, ripe but firm pineapple. Cut it into ¾-in/1.5-cm slices. Using a small plain cutter, remove the core of the pineapple. Select a larger cutter to remove the outer skin.

3

Coat with almond flakes or desiccated coconut and then shallow fry in butter or oil, until a golden colour. Drain on kitchen paper (paper towel).

2

Lightly flour the pineapple slices, and then dip in beaten egg.

4

Serve plain, or fill the centre hole with strawberry or maraschino cherry slices, or a fresh herb sprig.

VARIATION Apples can be prepared in the same way.

Frosted Cranberries

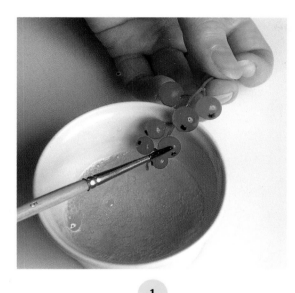

1

Select ripe cranberries, or other red berries, and separate into small bunches. Brush with beaten egg white.

3

Form into small clusters and leave on a wire rack to dry thoroughly.

2

Lightly sprinkle the fruit with caster (superfine) sugar.

4

Arrange the clusters, tucking a couple of small mint leaves in between them.

VARIATION The same method can be applied to black and green grapes, and, if used for decorating a dessert, dredge heavily with the sugar.

USE AS A GARNISH FOR:

TERRINES AND PÂTÉS

COLD MEAT PLATTERS

ROAST TURKEY AND GAME BIRD DISHES

CHEESEBOARDS

29

Star Fruit (Carambola)

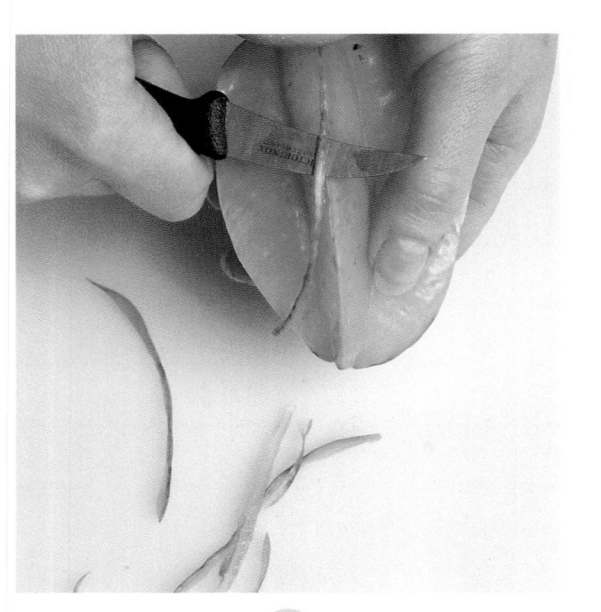

1

The unique shape of this fruit makes it a natural garnish.

Select a fruit which does not have too many blemishes. If necessary, finely pare down the points of the star to remove discoloured or rough skin.

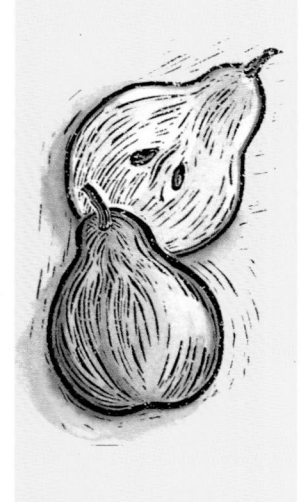

2

Slice the fruit approximately ¼ in/5 mm thick.

3

Use the sliced star fruit on its own, or with another fruit such as kiwi, or form into a flower using chive stems and herb leaves to make up the picture.

GARNISHING WITH SALAD VEGETABLES

Carrot & Cucumber Curls

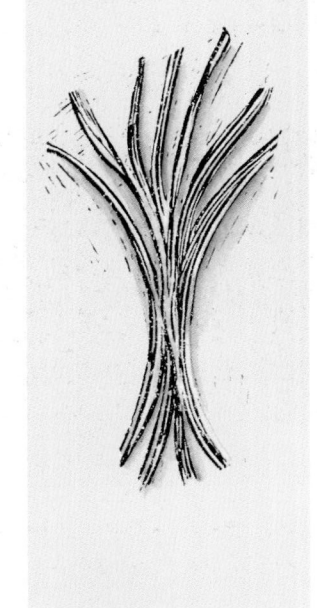

1

Select young vegetables – bright in colour and of a good straight shape. With a vegetable peeler, peel away fine, even strips. For cucumber curls, only the dark green skin can be used. Carrot curls can be made from the whole vegetable.

3

Alternatively, pack tightly into ice cube trays or plastic egg containers. Cover with cold water and then position the bowl or trays in the coldest part of the refrigerator for 6–24 hours.

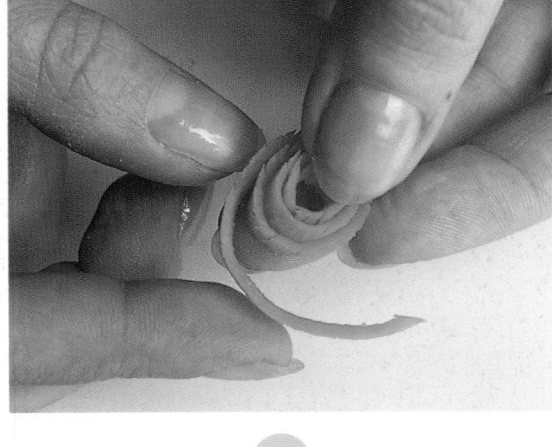
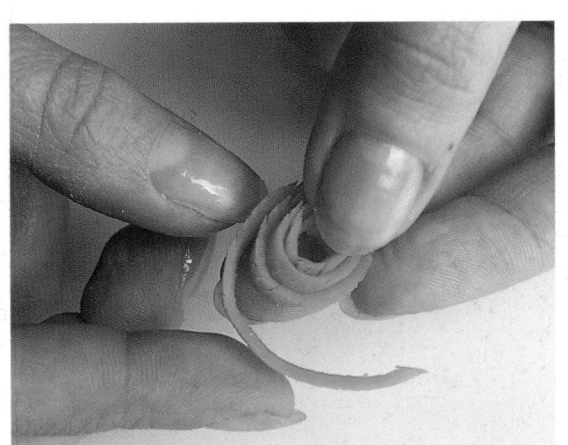

2

Roll up the slices, secure with a cocktail stick and put in a bowl.

4

Drain away the water, discard the cocktail sticks and gently uncoil the rolls to form attractive curls.

Chiffonade	**Chilli Flowers**

1

Thoroughly wash the large, outer leaves of a crisp lettuce, like iceberg or Webbs. Lay the leaves on top of each other and then tightly roll up to form a cigar shape. With a sharp knife, slice the lettuce very finely.

1

The stalk ends of small red or green chilli peppers are used for this garnish. Cut to the desired length. Slide a small paring knife around the inside of the chilli to loosen the core and seeds and remove them.

USE AS A GARNISH FOR:

CLEAR SOUPS AND CONSOMMÉS

CHIFFONADE IS A CLASSIC GARNISH FOR LIGHT SOUPS

2

Place the shredded lettuce in a colander or sieve and pour freshly boiled water over to blanch it. Refresh under cold water.

2

Using scissors, cut around the length of the chilli to form petals, trimming the tips of each petal to a point.

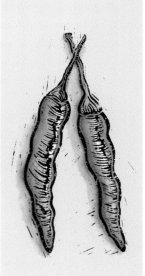

3

Sprinkle the lettuce chiffonade over the soup just before serving.

3

Drop the chilli flowers into iced water and leave for 1–1½ hours to allow the chilli flowers to 'blossom'.

CHILLI FLOWERS

USE AS A GARNISH FOR:

TERRINES, PÂTÉS AND MOUSSES

HOT, SPICY DISHES (MEXICAN AND THAI IN PARTICULAR)

Feathery Cucumber Fans & Fleurs-de-Lys

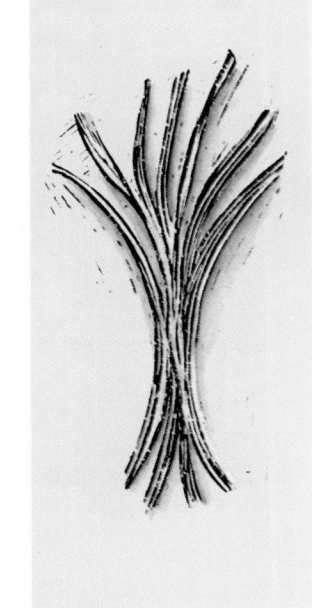

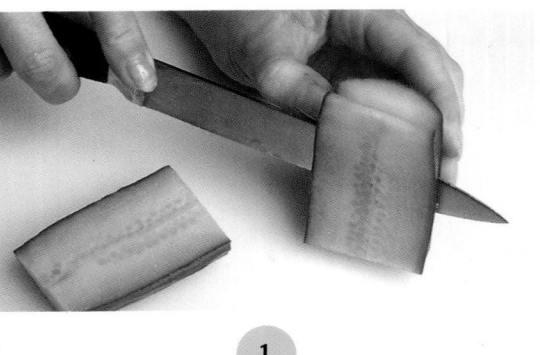

1

For a **Feathery Cucumber Fan,** cut a 3-in/8-cm piece from a length of cucumber. Cut this in half lengthwise. Then make a lengthwise cut along one of the halves deep enough to remove the seeds.

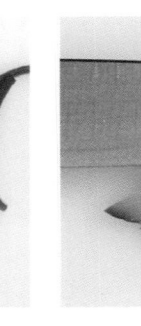

2

Using a sharp paring knife or grooving tool, cut out V-shaped grooves along the length of the outside of the cucumber.

3

Lay the cucumber on its flat base and, with a sharp knife, diagonally cut a corner off one end of the cucumber. Use the remaining pointed corner as the tip of the fan.

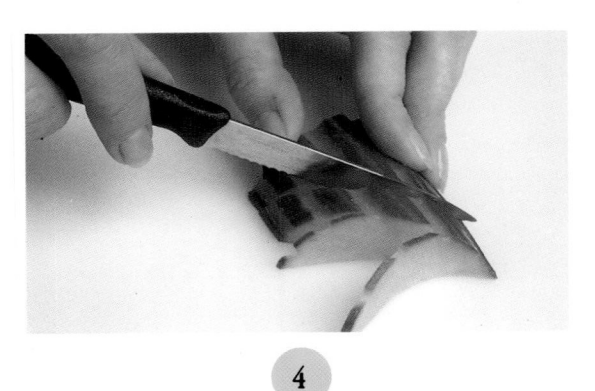

4

Cut five to ten paper-thin slices to the tip of the cucumber (as shown), taking care not to cut right through the tip. On the final slice cut right through to separate the fan from the remaining cucumber.

5

Using the flat side of the knife blade, gently press the cucumber slices so that they 'fan' out.

1

A **Cucumber Fleur-de-Lys** is made by following the steps above to make a seven-slice fan. Then, bend the second, fourth and sixth slice towards the joined end of the fan, forming small plumes. Arrange the fleur-de-lys, fold side down.

Radish Bud & Marguerite

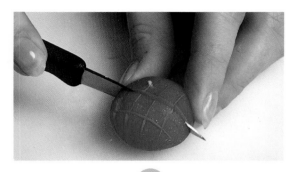

1

1

To make a **Radish Bud,** select a round, unblemished radish. Wash and cut a fine slice off the stalk end. Turn the radish over. Using a sharp paring knife, make 4 vertical and 6 horizontal cuts, stopping just short of the base of the radish – do not slice right through it.

To make a **Radish Marguerite,** initially prepare a radish as for a bud, then, using a small sharp paring knife, cut 4–6 leaf-shapes, into the red skin only, from the top centre almost down to the stalk end. Ease the red 'petals' away with the knife point, leaving the lower ends attached.

2

2

Drop the radish 'bud' into iced water, where it will take from 30 minutes to an hour to begin to open.

Drop the radish 'marguerite' into iced water where it will take from 30 minutes to an hour to begin to open.

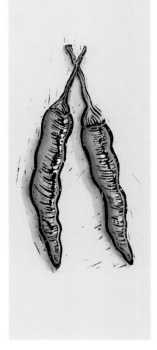

Green, Red & Yellow Peppers

USE AS A GARNISH FOR:

HORS D'OEUVRES AND CANAPÉS

ASPIC DISHES

TERRINES, PÂTÉS AND MOUSSES

EGG DISHES

COLD MEAT DISHES

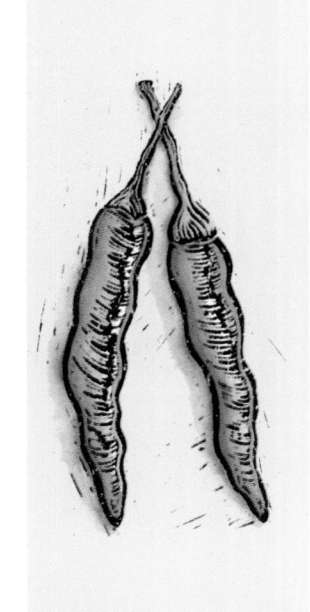

1

The bright, shiny skins of these sweet peppers are ideal for making into decorative shapes, and add instant colour to many dishes.

To prepare the peppers, wipe and then cut off a fairly thick slice at the stalk end.

2

Remove the white pith and seeds with a knife. Now the pepper can be sliced either across, or lengthwise, and made into all kinds of fancy shapes.

GHERKIN (DILL PICKLE) FANS

USE AS A
GARNISH FOR:

PÂTÉS, TERRINES
AND MOUSSES

EGG AND MEAT
DISHES

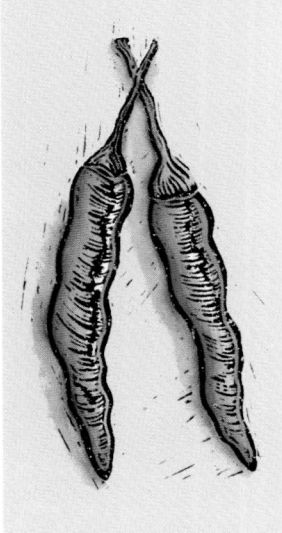

SPRING
ONION
FLOWERS

USE AS A
GARNISH FOR:

PÂTÉS, TERRINES
AND MOUSSES

CHINESE AND
ORIENTAL
COOKERY

MEAT DISHES

SALADS AND
VEGETABLE DISHES

Gherkin (Dill Pickle) Fans

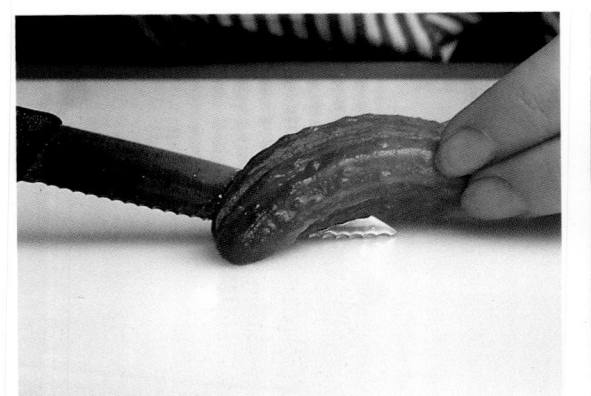

1

Drain the gherkins well. Make five parallel incisions through the length of the gherkin, but do not cut right down to the end.

2

Press the slices apart with the flat side of a knife blade to form a fan. Lay a fine strip of red canned pimento around the neck of the gherkin fan, to form a decorative band.

Spring Onion (Scallion) Flowers

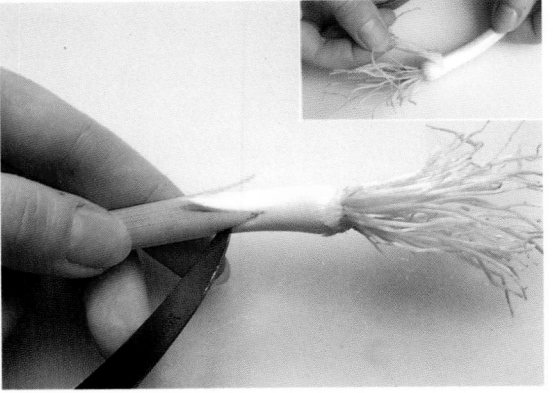

1

Select spring onions (scallions) with good-sized bulbs (the root end). Wash and remove the coarse outer leaves.

With a sharp paring knife, make 4–5 adjoining V-shaped cuts around each onion, through to the centre of the bulb.

2

Gently separate the carved stem (or bulb) end from the remaining onion (which can be used to make bows, or in salads). Carefully separate the petals of the flower with the tip of the knife or your fingers. Drop the spring onion flowers into iced water where within an hour they will begin to 'blossom'.

VARIATION Small shallots or pickling onions can be used instead of spring onions (scallions).

Spring Onion (Scallion) Curls & Bows

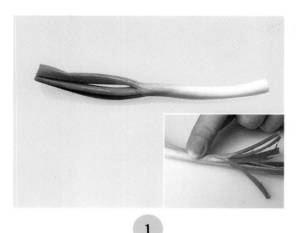

1

1

To make **Spring Onion (Scallion) Curls,** select medium-sized spring onions (scallions). Trim off the roots and remove any coarse outer leaves. Cut the onion to approximately 4 in/10 cm in length.

With a sharp knife, make a cut down the length of the spring onion to within 1½ in/4 cm of the root end. Rotate the onion a quarter turn and make another cut down the stem. (If you hold the onion stem firmly between your thumb and first finger, this will make it easier.)

Continue making as many fine cuts down the stem as possible, to form thin strands. Repeat with the remaining onions.

For **Spring Onion (Scallion) Bows,** select medium-sized spring onions and remove any coarse outer leaves. Trim the root and first ½ in/1 cm of the bulb end. Cut the onion to approximately 4 in/10 cm in length.

To form bows, make the cuts from both ends of the spring onion to within 1 in/2 cm of the centre. As with the Spring Onion Curl, rotate the onion and continue making fine cuts to produce a 'bowtie' effect.

2

Drop the onions into cold water, and refrigerate. In between 30 minutes and an hour the onions will have curled.

Tomato Crabs

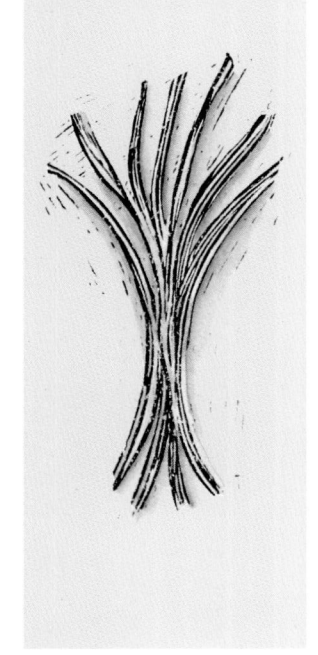

1

Sit a firm, ripe tomato on its stem end. Starting at one side, slice the tomato at approximately ¼-in/5-mm intervals, but do not cut right through to the base.

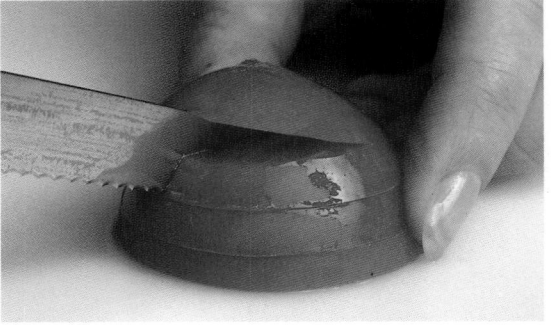

3

Lay the joined tomato slices, skin sides up, on the work surface. Gently lift up the top slice and, with a small knife, cut through the centre of the remaining slices.

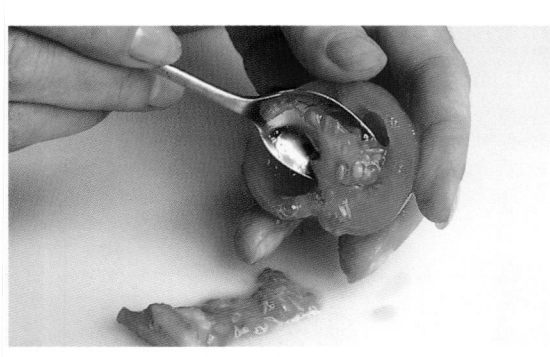

2

On the fourth slice, cut right through to separate the joined slices from the other half of the tomato. Using a teaspoon, scoop out the seeds.

4

Using the flat side of a knife blade, gently press the tomato slices out to form a crab. Repeat this procedure with the other side of the tomato to form a second crab.

Tomato Rose

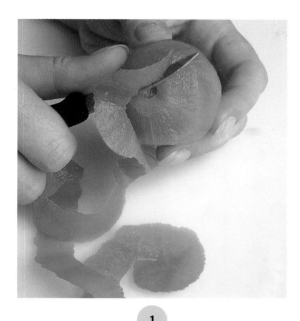

1

Select medium-sized, firm, ripe tomatoes. Starting at the non-stalk end of the tomato, slice a continuous paper-thin strip of skin ½ in/1.5 cm wide. Use a small sharp paring knife and cut in a circular fashion around the tomato to produce this 'spiral' with ease.

2

Using the stem end of the strip to form the centre of the rose, carefully wind the tomato peel around itself, skin side out.

3

When completely wound, shape the skin into a rose, making the 'petals' more open around the base of the flower. A couple of bay or mint leaves add a final touch.

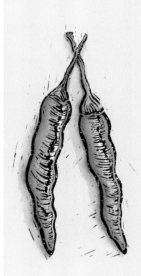

Tomato Tulip

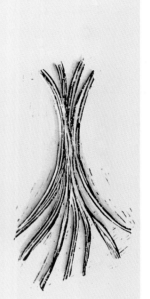

1

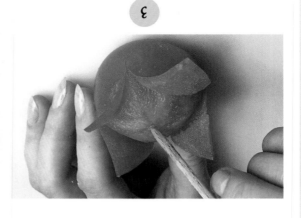

Without cutting into the tomato, score the skin into quarters from the top to two-thirds down.

2

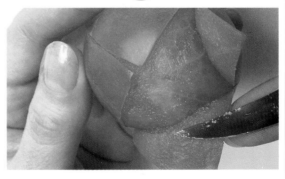

Using a paring knife, carefully peel back each 'petal' by cutting between the tomato skin and the flesh to about half the height of the tomato.

3

Gently pierce the top centre of the tomato with a wooden skewer to make a small hole.

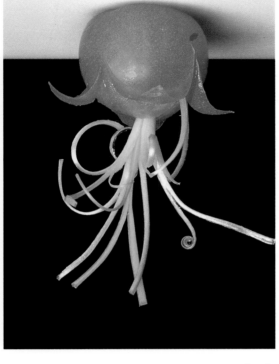

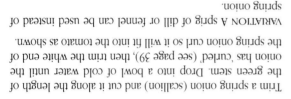

4

Trim a spring onion (scallion) and cut it along the length of the green stem. Drop into a bowl of cold water until the onion has 'curled' (see page 39), then trim the white end of the spring onion curl so it will fit into the tomato as shown.
VARIATION A sprig of dill or fennel can be used instead of spring onion.

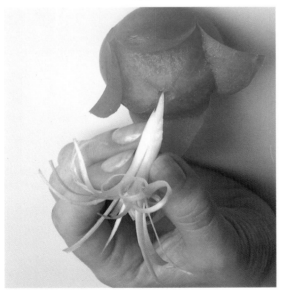

Onion Rings

1

Select firm, medium-sized red, white or brown onions. Peel off the outer papery skin. Turn the onion on its side and cut slices approximately ¼ in/5 mm thick. Separate the slices.

2

Sprinkle the rings with paprika pepper, turmeric or mild curry powder. Alternatively, toss the rings in finely chopped parsley, so that they are evenly coated.

Onion Chrysanthemum

1

Select a small, firm, white or red onion. Peel away the fine paper skin. Trim away the stem and the root.

Sit the onion firmly on its base and, with a small, sharp knife, make a series of criss-cross incisions, at approximately ¼ in/5 mm intervals. Do not cut right the way through to the root.

2

Let some of the onion pieces fall away (they can be discarded). Gently tease apart the onion to form a tight chrysanthemum flower.

3

Arrange singly, or in a group with a couple of bay leaves.

VARIATION If wished, the edge of the onion can be 'blushed' pink with a little food colouring. Shallots and pickling onions can also be used to make miniature chrysanthemums.

ONION RINGS

USE AS A GARNISH FOR:

TERRINES

MIDDLE EASTERN OR OTHER SPICY DISHES

VEGETABLE AND EGG DISHES

COLD MEAT PLATTERS

SALADS

ONION CHRYSANTHEMUM

USE AS A GARNISH FOR:

TERRINES AND PÂTÉS

COLD MEATS

FLANS

PIES

SALADS

White Radish Flower (Daikon or Mooli)

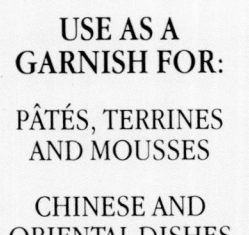

**USE AS A
GARNISH FOR:**

PÂTÉS, TERRINES
AND MOUSSES

CHINESE AND
ORIENTAL DISHES

COLD MEATS

SALADS

VEGETABLE DISHES

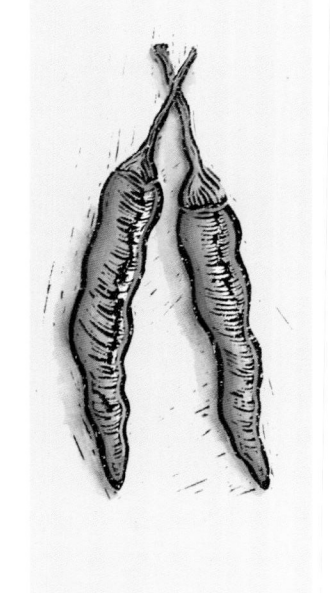

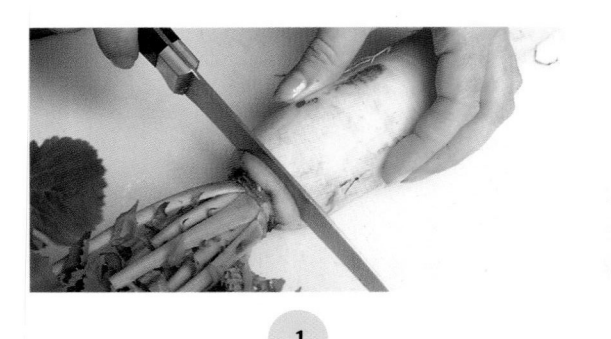

1

Cut off the leafy stem, and trim away the large leaves.

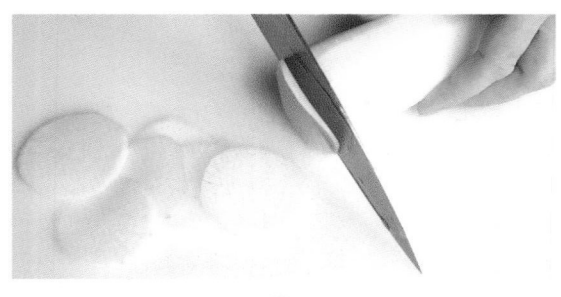

2

Soak the small inner leaves in a bowl of cold water.

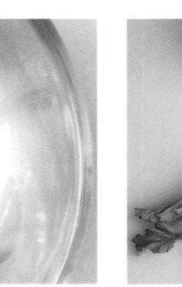

3

Peel the white radish, and for each flower cut three paper-thin slices.

4

Soak the slices in salted water for 30 minutes – by which time they will have become pliable.

5

Cut each slice halfway across to the centre. Overlap the cut sides slightly, as shown, and bend back half of the opposite edge to form a petal.

6

Once all three slices have been folded, arrange them together, one on top of the other, to form an open flower. Tuck a sprig or two of the drained inner leaves under the flower.

NOTE For a much bigger flower – as a centrepiece on a meat platter, for example – use eight slices of a larger white radish, forming each 'petal' into a saucer shape.

VEGETABLE GARNISHES

Asparagus Tips with Parma Ham

USE AS A GARNISH FOR:

SAVOURY MOUSSES, PÂTÉS AND VEGETABLE TERRINES

EGG DISHES

COLD MEAT AND FISH PLATTERS

OR ON TOASTS AS INDIVIDUAL CANAPÉS

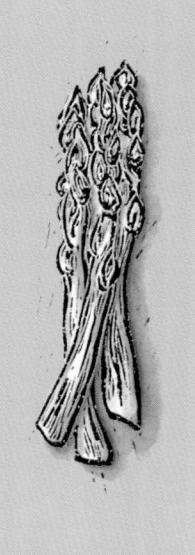

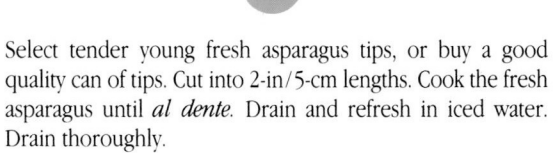

1

Select tender young fresh asparagus tips, or buy a good quality can of tips. Cut into 2-in/5-cm lengths. Cook the fresh asparagus until *al dente*. Drain and refresh in iced water. Drain thoroughly.

3

Lay the asparagus rolls on their seam and lightly glaze with some aspic jelly (see page 76) or gelatine dissolved in stock or wine.

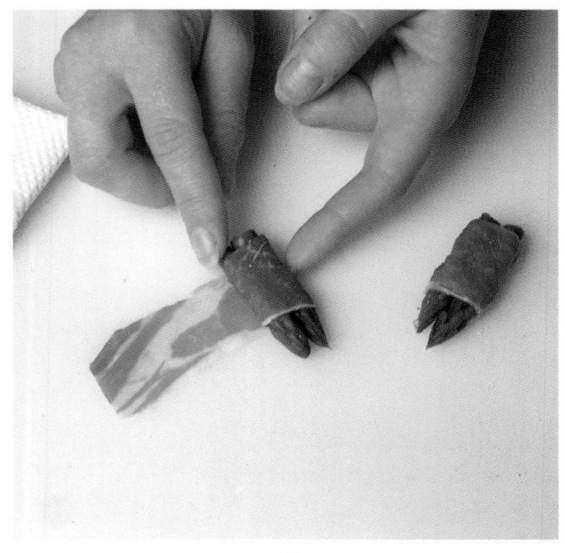

2

Cut the Parma ham into strips long enough to wrap around one or two asparagus tips twice, and cover two-thirds of the length of asparagus, revealing just the tip.

4

Garnish each roll with a bow made from a small strand of fresh chive or canned pimento, or with tiny hard-boiled egg shapes and red or black caviar or lumpfish roe.

46

Deep-fried Celery Leaves

1

Select a leafy green head of celery. Discard any tough outer leaves and remove the stalks. Detach small sprigs of leaves and, if necessary, wash and dry them.

3

Drain on absorbent kitchen paper (paper towel) and, with a pair of scissors, snip away the stalks just to below the first leaves.

2

Preheat some oil for deep-fat frying to 375°F/190°C. Drop the sprigs of leaves into the hot oil and fry for 1–2 minutes or until the leaves are golden brown and crisp. (Remove by the stalks as the leaves are brittle.)

4

Sprinkle the leaves lightly with paprika pepper to give a warm red dusting. Long, thin strands of cucumber also make an attractive addition. Use for garnish immediately.

USE AS A
GARNISH FOR:

GRILLED (BROILED)
MEATS AND FISH

ROAST JOINTS

EGG AND
VEGETABLE DISHES

Courgette (Zucchini) Barges

1

Select large-sized green courgettes (zucchini). Split each in half lengthwise, and then cut into 3-in/7-cm lengths. Using a small, sharp paring knife, carve the ends to form a barge shape.

2

Take a fine slice off the underside to give the 'barge' a secure base to sit on. With a small teaspoon or grapefruit knife, hollow out the courgette barge to within ¼ in/5 mm of the edge. Prepare the remaining wedges of courgette in the same way.

3

Prepare some tiny colourful vegetables – carrots, baby sweetcorn slices, baby mushroom slices, petit pois. Blanch the courgette barges and vegetables in boiling, salted water until *al dente*. Drain and toss in butter if to be presented as a hot garnish.

4

Fill the courgette barges with a cargo of vegetables and some tiny, fresh herb sprigs. The barges can be glazed with aspic (see page 76) if to be served cold.

Curly Tops

1

Select small tender beetroot (beet) or white radish (daikon). Trim away most of the leafy green part of the stem, leaving approximately 5 in/12 cm. Slice through the beetroot just 2 in/5 cm below the stem base, so that the garnish will sit firmly.

2

With a small sharp knife, make small diagonal incisions along the length of each stem.

3

Then slice through each stem lengthwise, to within 1 in/2.5 cm of the base. (Each stem will now be divided into two.)

4

Soak the stems in a bowl of iced water. In a short while, they will curl up to make an attractive garnish.

49

Green Laces

USE AS A GARNISH FOR:

SOUPS

EGG AND
VEGETABLE DISHES

GRILLED (BROILED)
MEAT AND FISH

CASSEROLES AND
SAUCES

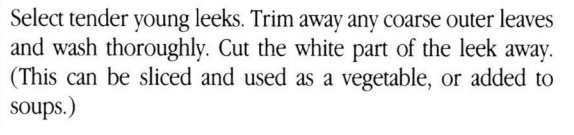

1

Select tender young leeks. Trim away any coarse outer leaves and wash thoroughly. Cut the white part of the leek away. (This can be sliced and used as a vegetable, or added to soups.)

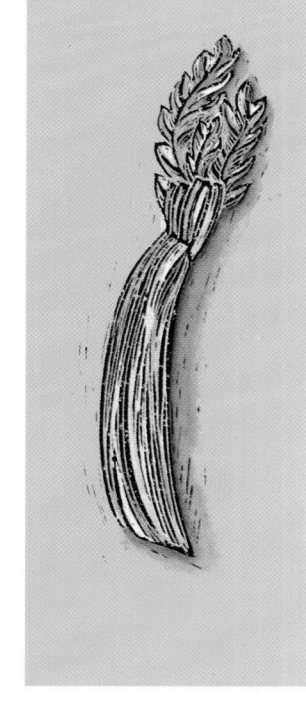

2

With a sharp, pointed knife, halve the leek lengthways. Then separate the layers and cut them lengthways into 'laces' ¼ in/5 mm wide.

3

Blanch the 'laces' in a pan of boiling salted water for 30–40 seconds. Drain and glaze with a knob of butter, if to be served as a hot garnish, otherwise, refresh in iced water and drain thoroughly.

Turned Mushroom Caps

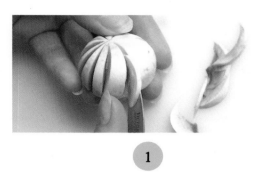

1

Select fresh, white, medium-sized button mushrooms. Wipe them clean with a damp cloth.

Hold the mushroom stem in one hand, and the blade of a sharp paring knife between the first finger and thumb of the other hand. Repeatedly draw the knife down from the centre to the base of the mushroom cap in a curved, sickle fashion. On each groove ensure that each alternate cut is at a flatter angle so that the piece of flesh will cleanly come away.

2

Trim the stalk and drop each mushroom into a bowl of water with a little lemon juice added to prevent discoloration while you prepare the rest.

3

The drained mushrooms can either be sautéed in butter, or used raw as a garnish.

Potato Allumettes

1

Allumettes is the French word for 'matches', a perfect description of this potato garnish.

Peel and thinly slice (approx. ⅛ in/3 mm) some firm, waxy potatoes. Trim the stacked slices into an even oblong or square 1½ in/4 cm in length. Slice through the potatoes at ⅛-in/3-mm intervals to produce the matchsticks.

Soak in cold water for at least 30 minutes. Drain and dry thoroughly.

2

Deep fry in hot oil (375°F/190°C) for just a few minutes or until a dark golden colour.

3

Drain on absorbent kitchen paper (paper towel), sprinkle with salt and serve immediately.

TURNED
MUSHROOM
CAPS

**USE AS A
GARNISH FOR:**

SAUTÉED FOR ALL
MEAT AND POULTRY
DISHES

EGG, RICE AND
PASTA DISHES

RAW WITH PÂTÉS,
SALADS, COLD MEAT
OR POULTRY DISHES

POTATO
ALLUMETTES

**USE AS A
GARNISH FOR:**

HOT GAME AND
MEAT DISHES

GRILLED (BROILED)
MEAT AND FISH
DISHES

Potato Baskets & Nests

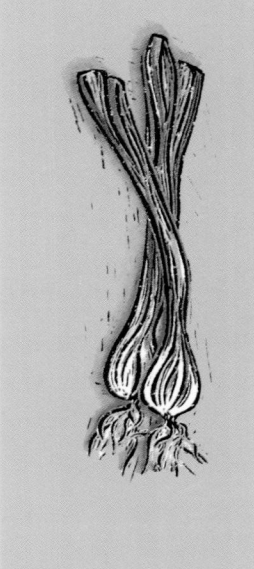

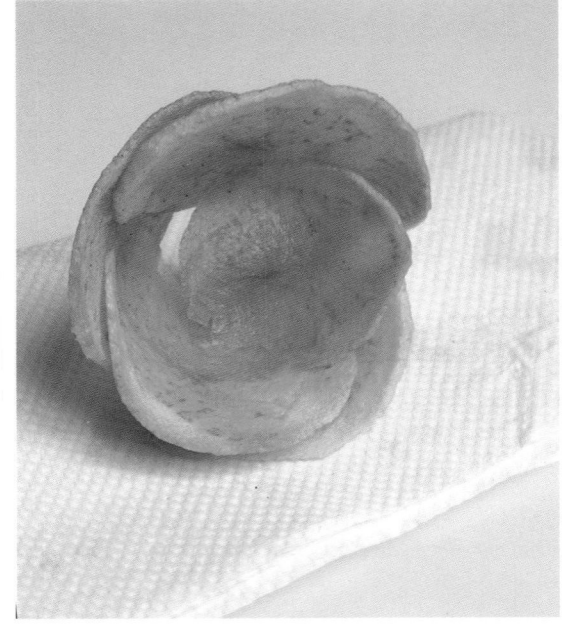

1

For **Potato Baskets**, peel and very thinly slice some firm, waxy potatoes. A vegetable peeler will produce fine, even slices. For **Potato Nests**, shred the potatoes or cut in fine straws. Soak the potato in cold water for 30 minutes. Drain and dry thoroughly.

Dip a special hinged frying basket into some hot oil to prevent the potatoes from sticking. Remove and line the frying basket with either over-lapping slices of potato or the shredded or straw potatoes.

3

Make up the quantity of baskets or nests required and then either reheat them in a hot oven 400°F/200°C/Gas 6 or by carefully refrying as above until a dark golden colour.

2

Deep fry the potato basket or nest in hot oil (350°F/180°C) until a light golden colour. Remove and drain the frying basket. Allow to cool slightly before carefully removing the cooked potato.

4

Serve immediately, filled with baby mushrooms, onions, glazed or puréed vegetables, or Bacon Rolls (see page 79).

Parisienne Potato Balls

1

Sieve some cooked mashed potato. Beat in one egg yolk for each 1 lb/500 g potatoes. Season with salt, pepper and a little freshly grated nutmeg.

2

Take a spoonful of the potato mixture and roll it between lightly floured hands to form a smooth round ball the size of a cherry. To ensure even-sized balls, it is a good idea to measure or weigh each spoonful of potato. Repeat the procedure until you have sufficient balls.

3

Dip each potato ball in beaten egg.

4

Using two forks coat the balls in fine dried breadcrumbs. Alternatively, after coating with the egg, roll the potato balls in flaked almonds or chopped hazelnuts.

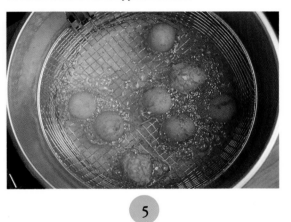

5

Deep-fat fry (350°F/180°C) until golden brown. Drain on absorbent kitchen paper (paper towel). Keep warm until required.

USE AS A GARNISH FOR:

HOT MEAT, GAME, CHICKEN AND FISH DISHES – PARTICULARLY GRILLED (BROILED) AND ROAST CUTS

ALSO AS A VEGETABLE ACCOMPANIMENT

Julienne Bundles

1

Choose a colourful assortment of vegetables, such as courgette (zucchini), carrot, celery, green beans and swede (rutabaga). Trim, peel and cut into thin strips – *à la julienne*—approximately 2½ in × ¼ in × ¼ in/6 cm × 5 mm × 5 mm.

2

Blanch the julienne vegetables in a pan of boiling water for 1 minute. Drain and glaze with a little butter if to be served hot; alternatively, refresh in iced water and drain.

3

Form the assorted vegetables julienne into small bundles and secure together with an onion ring or a fine chive stem tied in a knot.

Vegetable Coils

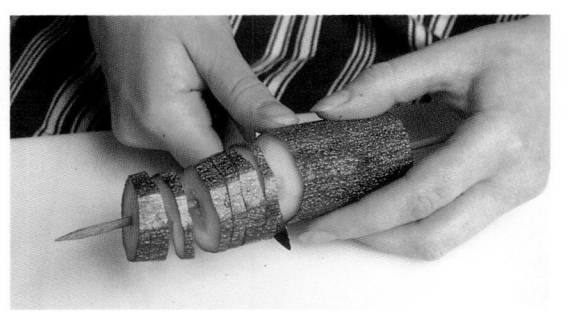

1

Select small, tender vegetables which are straight in shape. Carrots, cucumbers, courgettes (zucchini) and small white radishes (mooli or daikon) are all suitable for this garnish. If using carrots or courgettes, boiling them first until *al dente* and then refresh in iced water, to make them a little more tender and pliable to work with.

Trim to 3–4 in/8–10 cm in length. Insert either a wooden skewer or chopstick through the centre of the vegetable from end to end.

With a small, sharp knife, starting at approximately ¼ in/5 mm from the end of the vegetable, slice through to the wooden skewer. Firmly holding the knife at a slight angle, turn the vegetable and continue cutting around the wooden skewer, in a spiral action, until the end is reached.

2

Remove the skewer and gently tease apart the vegetable to form a decorative coil.

VARIATION If wished, the centre of the cucumber or courgette can be easily scooped out to produce a more delicate-looking coil.

BREAD & PASTRY GARNISHES

Crispy Bread Cases

1

Trim the crusts from a slightly stale, large, white tin loaf (one to two-days old). Cut the bread into 2-in/5-cm slices. Score ½ in/1 cm in from the edge all the way round the bread, and to within ½ in/1 cm of the base.

3

Place the cases on a well-buttered baking tray. With a pastry brush, liberally coat the surfaces of the case with melted butter.

Bake in a preheated oven at 325°F/170°C/Gas 3 for about 1 hour, or until crisp and golden.

2

Hollow out the centre section, using a sharp knife. Shake out any loose crumbs remaining in the case.

4

Fill the warm bread case with sautéed mushrooms, baby onions, mixed or puréed vegetables and fresh herbs.

NOTE The bread cases can be deep fried, if preferred.

Golden Breadcrumbs

1 Use day-old bread to make wholemeal or white breadcrumbs. Either use a blender/liquidizer or food processor for speedy results.

For every 1 cup/50 g/2 oz breadcrumbs use 2 tbsp/25 g/2 tbsp unsalted butter, plus 1 tbsp/15 ml/1 tbsp vegetable oil. Heat the fat in a frying pan until it starts to foam.

2 When the foaming begins to subside, toss in the breadcrumbs, reduce the heat to low and stir the crumbs continually to cook them to a dark golden colour.

Serve the breadcrumbs warm, in a small dish or sprinkle around your chosen meat.

Cheese Profiteroles

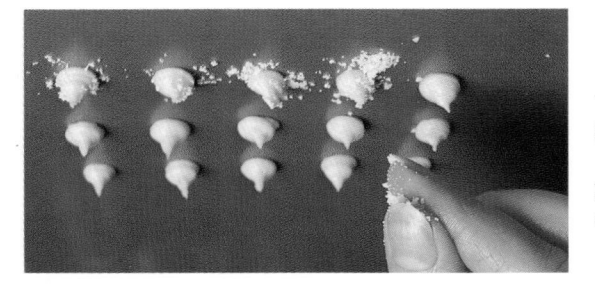

1 Using choux paste (see page 109), pipe out mounds the size of a pea onto a damp baking tray.

2 Sprinkle with some freshly grated Parmesan cheese.

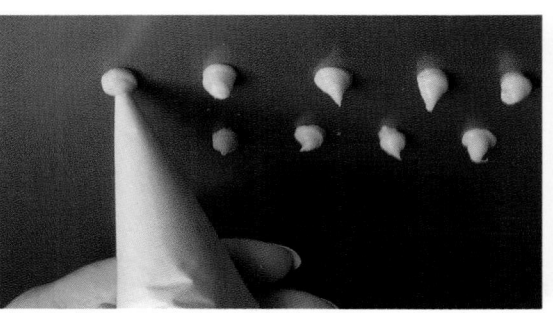

3 Bake in a preheated oven at 425°F/220°C/Gas 7 for 6–10 minutes, or until golden and crisp.

Immediately before serving, float several profiteroles on each serving of soup.

GOLDEN
BREADCRUMBS

USE AS A
GARNISH FOR:

ROAST GAME –
PHEASANT,
PARTRIDGE, WILD
DUCK ETC.

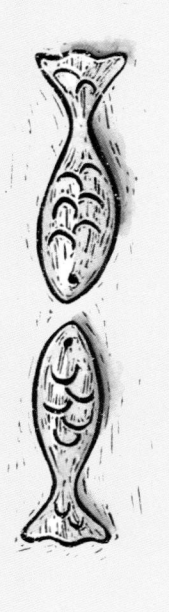

CHEESE
PROFITEROLES

USE AS A
GARNISH FOR:

CONSOMMÉS AND
CLEAR SOUPS
OR AS CANAPÉS

Croûtons & Croûtes

1

Trim away the crusts from thick slices of wholemeal or white bread. (One-day-old bread is more successful than fresh.) Cut the bread into ¼-in/5-mm cubes.

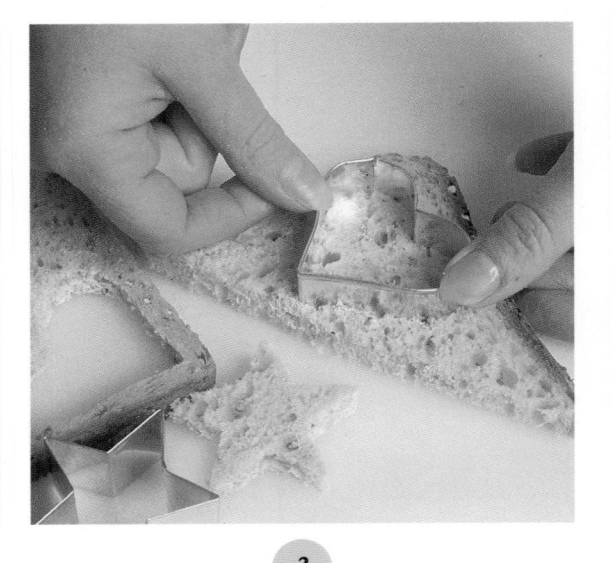

3

Larger heart, round or diamond shaped croûtes can be cooked in exactly the same way and use to garnish meat and chicken casseroles. Use pastry cutters to obtain the desired shape.

VARIATION Frying in flavoured butter, such as garlic, herb or peppered butter (see page 72 for some ideas) can add extra flavour to the croûtons or croûtes.

2

Heat an equal quantity of a good vegetable oil and unsalted butter. When the fat is foaming, toss in the croûtons and stir continuously, ensuring the cubes are evenly browned and cooked.

Drain the croûtons on several layers of absorbent kitchen paper (paper towel) before serving.

Poppadom Baskets

1

2

Buy small, round poppadoms – alternatively cut larger ones into smaller circles using scissors. Ideally, they should be 4–5 in/10–13 cm in diameter.

Heat some oil for deep-fat frying. Holding a metal ladle in one hand (or a small metal sieve) and a spoon in the other, hold the poppadom between the two utensils, and slowly lower into the hot oil.

Fry for just a few seconds, during which time the poppadom will curl up around the inner spoon, to form a shallow basket shape. When it is golden and crisp, remove from the hot oil, drain thoroughly and leave to cool on absorbent kitchen paper (paper towel).

Store the cooked poppadoms in an airtight container until required.

3

Fill with finely diced tomatoes, cucumber, sweet peppers or onions, and toasted, flaked or desiccated coconut before serving.

USE AS A GARNISH FOR:

HOT SPICY DISHES – CURRIES IN PARTICULAR

SALADS

Pastry Garnishes for Pies

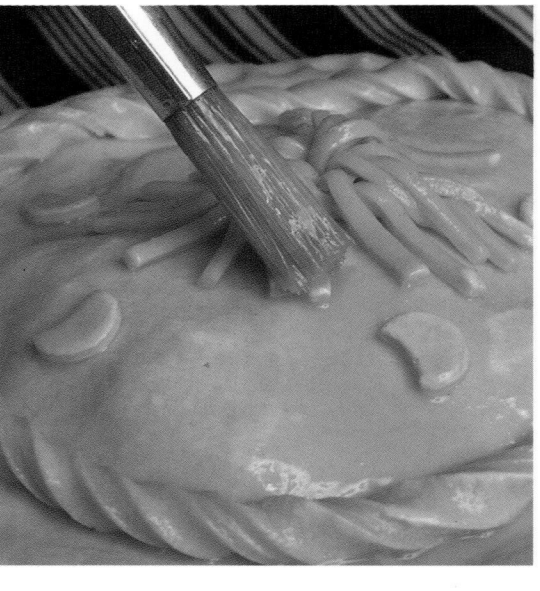

● A pastry-covered pie can be attractively garnished with the remaining pastry bits, to add the final touch to the dish.

● For fish or chicken pies, special cutters are available to make pastry fish and chicken shapes. Otherwise, use a sharp knife and shape your own animals!

● Refer to Pastry Fleurons (page 62) for some other ideas on shapes. These can then be brushed with a little water or egg glaze and positioned on the pie. Bake the pie according to your recipe (see right).

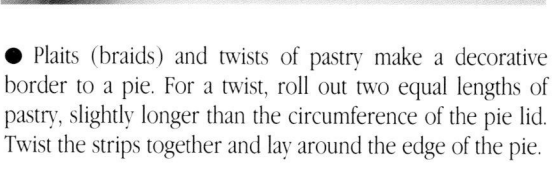

● Plaits (braids) and twists of pastry make a decorative border to a pie. For a twist, roll out two equal lengths of pastry, slightly longer than the circumference of the pie lid. Twist the strips together and lay around the edge of the pie.

● Pastry tassels make an ideal centrepiece. Cut a pastry strip 1 in/2.5 cm wide and about 6 in/15 cm long. Make cuts ¾ in/2 cm long at ¼-in/5-mm intervals, then roll up the strip. Place it on the pie and open out the tassels.

Pastry Fleurons

1

A good stand-by in the freezer are sheets of puff pastry which can be simply transformed into decorative shapes by using small cutters and a sharp knife.

Using a plain scone (biscuit) cutter, cut out crescents as shown. Heart shapes, letters, fish and star shapes can also be made with special cutters.

2

Mark and cut out square shapes; cut in half diagonally to form triangles. Using the back of a knife or skewer, mark on a criss-cross pattern. Cut out leaf shapes and mark the veins with back of a knife or skewer.

3

Lay the shapes on a damp baking tray, brush with an egg glaze and bake in a preheated oven at 400°F/200°C/Gas 6 for 7–10 minutes or until well risen, crisp and golden brown.

NOTE Pastry fleurons can be stored in the freezer in a rigid container until required. Thaw out and heat through before serving.

Choux Pastry Swans

1

Make up a quantity of unsweetened choux paste (see page 109). Fit a small piping bag with a small plain nozzle. Spoon in one-third of the choux paste.

Lightly grease a baking tray, and pipe out a swan's head and neck. This will require a little practice, but is made in two movements: the beak first, and then the head and neck, which is shaped like a figure 'S'. Repeat.

2

Using a star nozzle fitted in a second piping bag, use the remaining choux paste to form the swans' bodies. Piping in a circular movement, form an oblong, which is slightly higher at one end. Repeat.

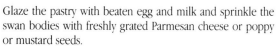

3

Glaze the pastry with beaten egg and milk and sprinkle the swan bodies with freshly grated Parmesan cheese or poppy or mustard seeds.

Cook at 400°F/200°C/Gas 6 for 15–20 minutes (the heads and necks will need less time), or until well risen and golden brown.

4

Cool the 'swans' before assembling. Split the bodies in half horizontally and then cut the top half of the body in half lengthwise to form two wings.

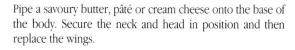

5

Pipe a savoury butter, pâté or cream cheese onto the base of the body. Secure the neck and head in position and then replace the wings.

Pastry Horns

1

Buy a good quality packet of rough puff or flaky pastry or filo pastry leaves. Thaw and refrigerate until required.

Lightly grease either the base end of some cream horn moulds, or homemade aluminium-foil moulds. Stuff them with crumpled foil so that they hold their shape. (The size of the horns will depend upon the dish they will garnish, but they do not want to be too big.)

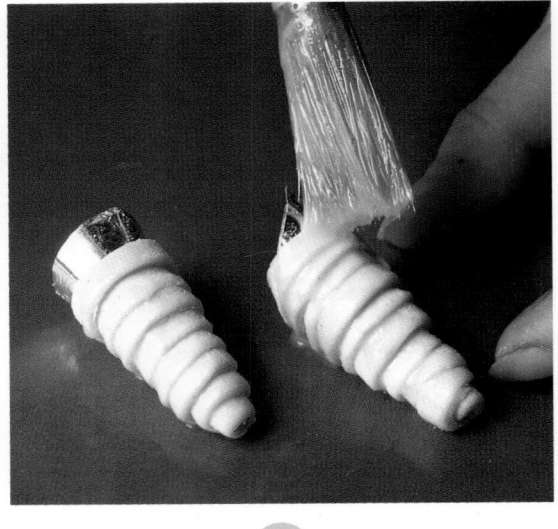

2

Thinly roll out the puff or flaky pastry on a lightly floured board. Trim the edges and cut into strips approximately ¼ in/5 mm wide.

Wind a strip of pastry round the mould in an overlapping coil. Dampen the loose end with a drop of water to secure it down.

3

Place the horns on a buttered baking sheet (with the loose end downwards). Glaze with beaten egg and milk. They can be sprinkled with sesame or poppy seeds if wished. Bake in a preheated oven at 425°F/220°C/Gas 7 for 10–15 minutes or until golden brown and crisp.

4

Slip the horns from their moulds and cool on a wire rack. Fill with smooth pâté, cream cheese or a vegetable purée, using a piping bag, and top with nuts or sliced stuffed olives, spices or herbs.

VARIATION Larger horns can be made and filled for a first course.

EGG GARNISHES

Chopped Egg Garnishes

USE AS A GARNISH FOR:

DRESSED CRAB

FISH AND SAVOURY FLANS

MOUSSES

SALADS AND RICE DISHES

MAYONNAISE-BASED DISHES

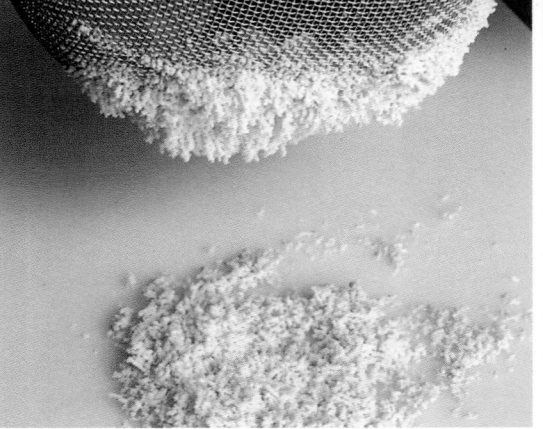

1

Hard-boil one or two eggs, starting them off in cold water and allowing them 10 minutes boiling time. Cool rapidly, then shell and separate the yolk from the white.

Pass the yolk through a metal sieve, pressing with a wooden spoon.

3

Use fine lines of alternating yellow yolk and the speckled green egg whites.

2

Finely chop the egg white and either leave plain or mix with finely chopped fresh parsley.

4

If preferred, the finely chopped parsley can be used as a third colour, with the plain egg yolk and egg white, or the white can be dusted with paprika.

Egg Flowers

1 Hard boil one or two eggs (see page 66), then plunge into cold water immediately.

Using a stainless steel knife, slice or halve the egg according to the garnish required. (The egg is most successfully sliced in an egg slicer —as shown—which will produce even, clean cut slices.)

2 The whites can then be cut into fancy shapes using aspic cutters, piping nozzles, and serrated knives.

3 Sieved egg yolk can act as the centre of the flower. Alternatively, cut out a round of yolk with a small, plain piping nozzle.

4 Blanched leek or cucumber peel can be used for bolder stem and leaf shapes. Chive stems and fine herb leaves will produce a more delicate garnish.

USE AS A GARNISH FOR:

TERRINES, PÂTÉS AND MOUSSES

COLD MEATS AND PIES

ASPIC-COATED DISHES

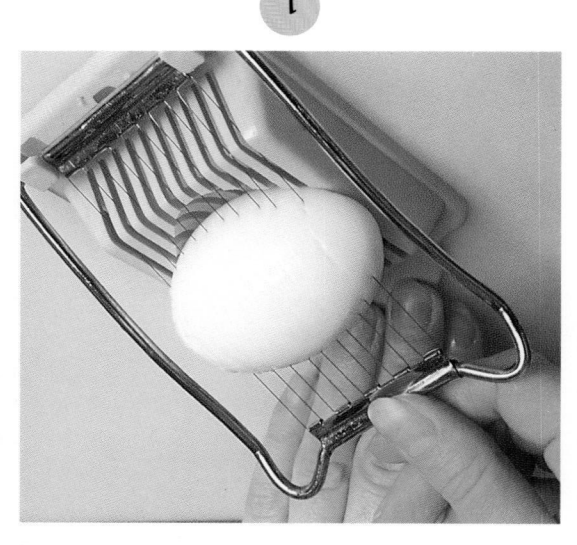

Egg Royale

USE AS A
GARNISH FOR:

CLEAR SOUPS AND
CONSOMMÉS

1

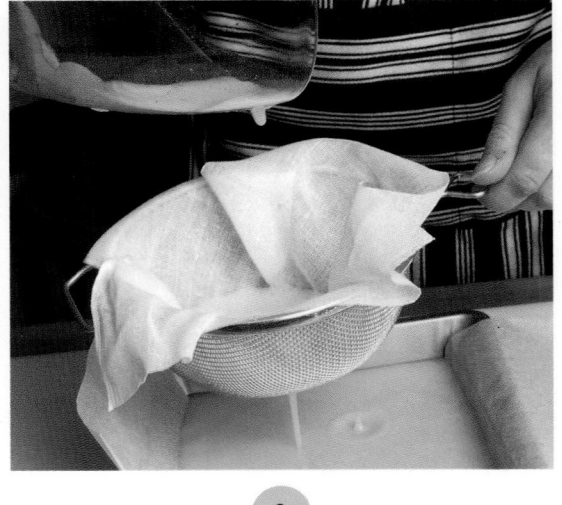

2

Beat together 3 eggs and 1 cup/250 ml/8 fl oz hot stock (broth) or consommé. Season lightly with salt and pepper.

Sieve the custard through a fine mesh or piece of muslin (cheesecloth) into a shallow tin, lined with greaseproof (waxed) paper.

Stand the tin in a roasting tin containing ½ in/1 cm water and cook in a pre-heated oven at 300°F/160°C/Gas 2 for 40–50 minutes, or until firm to the touch.

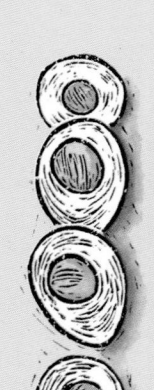

3

Cool, then carefully lift out the set custard using the greaseproof (waxed) paper lining as a cradle. Cut out fancy shapes using aspic and pastry cutters (dice, stars, moons, hearts).

VARIATION The custard can be coloured by adding 2 tbsp/30 ml/2 tbsp chopped spinach, watercress or tomato purée (paste).

Egg Strands

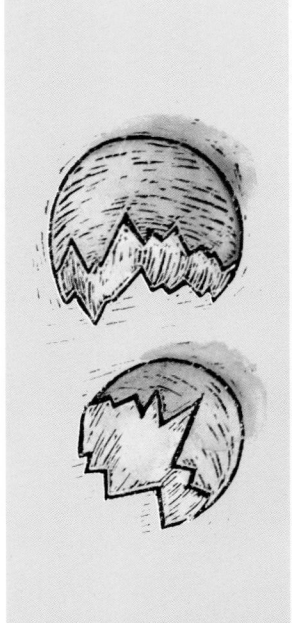

1

Have a clear consommé or Chinese soup which is gently simmering and ready to serve. Thoroughly beat an egg in a small jug with a good pouring lip.

2

Very slowly pour the egg onto the simmering soup. Simultaneously stir the egg in a figure of eight with a fork or skewer, which will help form very fine strands of cooked egg.

3

Serve the soup immediately, sprinkled with finely chopped spring onion (scallion) or freshly chopped herbs.

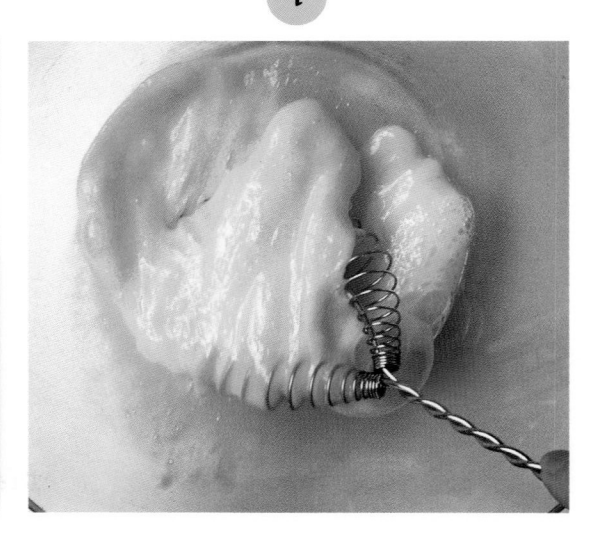

Shredded Pancakes (Crêpes)

1

Make a batter using 1 cup/125 g/4 oz plain flour, 3 eggs, ¼ cup/45 ml/3 tbsp vegetable oil. Leave to stand for 30 minutes to an hour, then add 2 tbsp/45 ml/2 tbsp finely chopped fresh herbs.

Cook a batch of thin pancakes (crêpes). Allow to cool and stack between layers of greaseproof (waxed) paper.

3

With a sharp knife, finely slice the pancake to form thin shreds. Warm through in the oven or microwave oven before sprinkling onto soups.

NOTE By making a batch of pancakes, any spare can be frozen between layers of greaseproof (waxed) paper and then thawed out individually for use as a garnish, when required.

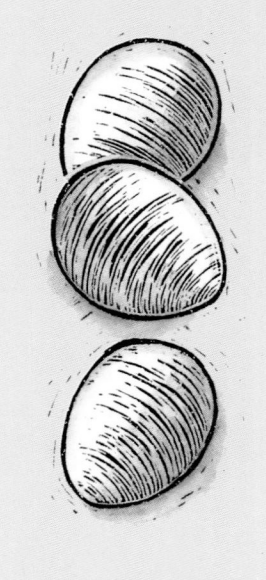

2

Tightly roll up a couple of stacked pancakes, to form a cigar shape.

BUTTER GARNISHES

Speciality Butters

1 Maître d'Hôtel Butter, **2** Tomato Butter, **3** Red Pepper Butter, **4** Mustard Butter, **5** Fresh Herb Butter, **6** Orange Butter, **7** Caper Butter.

As well as presenting butters attractively, as described in the following two garnishes, the butters can also be flavoured before forming into balls or curls or other shapes. Not only will the butter enrich and moisten the food but it will also coat the food with a delicious buttery lemon or herb flavour, for example. Here are a few ideas for flavouring butters before they are shaped or moulded:

● *Caper Butter*

To ½ cup/125 g/4 oz butter, add 1 tsp/5 ml/1 tsp crushed capers. Stir in ½ tsp/2.5 ml/½ tsp each orange and lemon juice and ¼ cup/50 g/2 oz drained finely chopped anchovies. Shape into balls and chill.

Use to garnish and accompany grilled (broiled) fish.

● *Orange Butter*

To ½ cup/125 g/4 oz butter, blend in 1 tbsp/15 ml/1 tbsp each finely grated orange rind, orange juice and green peppercorns. Spread in a ½ in/1 cm thick layer on foil and chill. Cut into rectangles for serving.

Use to garnish and accompany fish, pork, chicken and game, and boiled vegetables.

● *Red Pepper Butter*

To ½ cup/125 g/4 oz butter beat in a pinch of ground ginger and a few drops of Tabasco sauce. Mix 3 tbsp/45 ml/3 tbsp finely chopped sweet red pepper. Form into a long roll. Wrap in foil and chill. Unwrap, coat in finely chopped parsley and slice.

Use to garnish and accompany grilled (broiled) meats, fish, potatoes baked in their skins and vegetable dishes.

● *Mustard Butter*

To ½ cup/125 g/4 oz butter, beat in 1 tbsp/15 ml/1 tbsp mustard, 6 drops Tabasco sauce and a dash of Worcestershire sauce. When light and fluffy, transfer to a piping bag with small plain nozzle and pipe three blobs close together (trefoil shape) onto foil. Repeat. Chill well. Place a tiny herb sprig in the centre of each.

Use to garnish and accompany grilled (broiled) meats and fish.

● *Tomato Butter*

To ½ cup/125 g/4 oz butter beat in 2 tsp/10 ml/2 tsp tomato purée (paste). Chill, then form into balls.

Use to garnish and accompany hot meat, fish, vegetable and pasta dishes.

● *Fresh Herb Butter*

To ½ cup/125 g/4 oz butter blend in 1 tbsp/15 ml/1 tbsp freshly chopped mixed fresh herbs (chives, tarragon and parsley for example). Form into a roll. Wrap in foil and chill. Slice the butter.

Use to garnish and accompany hot meat, fish and vegetable dishes.

● *Maître d'Hôtel Butter*

To ½ cup/225 g/4 oz butter beat in 2 tbsp/30 ml/2 tbsp finely chopped fresh parsley and 1 tsp/5 ml/1 tsp lemon juice. Season with a little salt and freshly ground pepper. Form into an oblong. Wrap in foil and chill before serving.

Use to garnish and accompany grilled (broiled) steaks, fish and vegetable dishes.

Butter Balls

1

Butter balls can be made by two different methods. The first is to use a Parisienne cutter (melon baller) which has first been dipped in very hot water. Press the cutter into the firm butter and turn it firmly to produce a ball. Drop the ball into iced water until required.

2

Alternately, cut a piece of butter approximately 1 in/2.5 cm square and roll it between two wet butter pats to obtain a round ball. Drop the ball into icy water, as above.

3

The balls can either be served plain, or rolled in finely chopped fresh herbs, paprika, crushed coriander seeds, mixed peppercorns, or finely chopped toasted hazelnuts.

4

If the butter balls are to be used as an accompaniment to bread or biscuits (crackers), arrange the balls into a bunch of grapes. Approximately 30 or 40 balls will be needed to make an impressive bunch. The stem and leaf can be cut out of butter, or cucumber skin (see Melon 'Grapes' page 26).

USE AS A
GARNISH FOR:

HOT GRILLED
(BROILED) STEAKS
AND CHOPS

POTATOES BAKED IN
THEIR SKINS

VEGETABLES

73

Butter Curls

USE AS A GARNISH FOR:

GRILLED (BROILED) MEATS

VEGETABLES AND POTATOES

OR AS AN ATTRACTIVE WAY OF PRESENTING BUTTER TO ACCOMPANY BREAD, TOAST OR BISCUITS (CRACKERS)

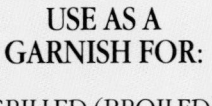

1

To obtain perfect butter curls, a special tool called a butter curler is required. Dip the butter curler in hot water before forming each curl.

Stand a well chilled block of butter on its side and firmly pull the butter curler along the length of butter, from end to end, to form the curl.

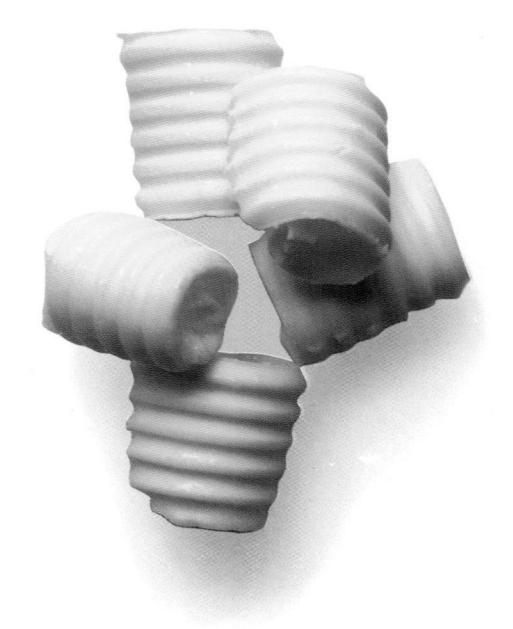

2

Drop the curl into a bowl of iced water until required.

MISCELLANEOUS GARNISHES

Aspic

Aspic is widely used to garnish foods – whether as a decorative glazed coating, a jellied mould, set and chopped to produce a sparkling border for foods, or used to line serving dishes with a thin glossy glaze.

Traditionally made from strong fish or meat stocks (broths), wine and seasonings, aspic is now available commercially, and can be easily made, following the manufacturer's instructions.

2

● Coarsely chop the set aspic with a knife to form sparkling crystals. Finely chopped herbs can be added to the nearly set jelly to produce an interesting variation.

1

● Set aspic can be cut into a variety of decorative shapes using special cutters.

3

● Coat galantines, pâtés, meat cutlets, savoury mousses and terrines with cool aspic. (This is best done on a wire cooling rack.)

Dip or brush decorative shapes with the aspic and arrange on the tops of mousses and terrines. Spoon a second coating of aspic over the mousse or terrine, if required.

Herbs

Herbs are becoming more readily available—either in the form of small sachets of freshly cut herbs (in large supermarkets) or growing from your own window box or herb garden. The choice of herb is entirely personal but certain herbs go particularly well with certain dishes, such as tarragon with chicken (see page 106) and rosemary with lamb.

● Once cut, fresh sprigs of herbs will keep fresh in an airtight plastic container stored in the bottom of the refrigerator.

● Chopped fresh herbs can be frozen for future use. Small ice cube trays are perfect for this, and the chopped herbs can be covered with water or vinegar (for mint sauce), frozen and then used in just the right quantity to add to a sauce or soup. (Whole sprigs of fresh herbs will not freeze successfully; they will wilt and lose their shape.)

● Just the tiniest sprig of herb is usually all that is needed to garnish a dish—'a tree, not a forest . . .' was advice given to heavy-handed cooks at college!

● Use the herb which has already been used in the recipe, or blends well with the ingredients and origin of the recipe (for example, coriander for Middle Eastern dishes, marjoram or basil for Mediterranean fare).

● Finely chopped herbs sprinkled over a dish can add instant colour and flavour to bland foods, and 'lifts' the plain boiled potato in an instant.

● Finely chopped herbs added to aspic (see page 76), and savoury butters (see page 72) are other ways of incorporating extra colour into dishes and their garnishes.

● Sprigs of parsley, dusted in flour, and deep-fat fried for just a few seconds (or until crisp) will give added interest to grilled (broiled) and fried meat and fish.

● Home-grown herbs not only offer an instant garnish or flavouring to a dish – but are also popular with the flower arranger! In the summer, the delicate, tiny flowers on many herbs are a picture in a small posy or vase. Herbs which have attractive flowers include thyme, mint, borage, savory, burnet, marjoram and oregano.

When the herbs are flowering, cut an assorted range, and form into miniature bouquets. The herbs can be 'tied' together with a stem of chive and then laid on the side of a plate as a unique but natural garnish.

● Access to fresh herbs is a cook's saving grace. If all else fails, the herb won't—and with very little preparation, it will bring life to practically every type of food in need of garnishing.

Nuts

Nuts – whether chopped, flaked, toasted or fried – offer an abundance of flavour, texture and colour and make an ideal garnish for many dishes.

Always select fresh nuts – once exposed to air, they do tend to lose their flavour and can go rancid quickly. Store in an airtight jar in the fridge, or longer still in the freezer.

● Toasted, flaked almonds make an attractive garnish for rice and curry dishes, giving a contrast in texture and colour. Brown the flaked almonds on a baking tray either in a hot oven or under the grill (broiler).

● Pistachio nuts are a delicate pale green in colour and have a sweet, pleasant flavour. They grow in pairs inside a thin husk, and can be used to garnish meat terrines and pâtés or Mediterranean dishes.

● Walnuts are probably the most commonly used nut in cooking. Whole, halved or finely chopped, they add flavour and are an attractive garnish to many salads, green vegetables and pâtés, and can even be finely chopped in savoury butters for fish.

● Pine nuts are delicious fried in butter and then sprinkled over Italian dishes and sauces, vegetables or salads or into spicy vegetable soups.

● Desiccated or flaked coconut, toasted, is traditionally used to garnish 'sambals', the accompaniments to curries. Sprinkled over a tomato salad, it offers both a flavour contrast and a crunchy texture. It is also delicious on some fish and vegetable dishes.

● Hazelnuts have a very distinct flavour and are most delicious toasted and skinned. Finely chopped, they make a crunchy coating for Parisienne Potato Balls (see page 53) and can be combined with breadcrumbs for use as a coating or sprinkled over vegetables. Flaked hazelnuts can also garnish soups and salads.

● Devilled nuts can be simply made by frying your favourite blanched nut (whole almonds are most successful) in oil and butter until browned, and then tossing them in salt and cayenne or curry powder. They can then be used for Eastern and spicy dishes.

Bacon Rolls

1

2

Select some good streaky bacon. Remove any rind and bones with a pair of scissors.

Cut each rasher (slice) of bacon into two or three pieces. With the blade of a sharp knife, held at an angle, stretch the bacon, using firm stroking movements.

Roll up each bacon slice and secure, if necessary, with a wooden cocktail stick. Cook the bacon rolls under a hot grill (broiler), turning frequently to ensure an even colour and crispness. Alternatively, bake in a preheated oven at 400°F/200°C/Gas 6.

USE AS A GARNISH FOR:

ROAST CHICKEN AND TURKEY

SMOKED HADDOCK DISHES

OMELETTES AND OTHER EGG DISHES

TOSSED IN GREEN SALADS

Crunchy Bacon Bits

1

2

Select good streaky bacon. Using a pair of scissors, cut away any rind and bones. Snip the bacon into small pieces.

Fry the bacon in its own fat in a non-stick pan, stirring frequently to ensure even cooking and colour. When the bacon bits are crunchy, drain on a piece of absorbent kitchen paper (paper towel) before using.

Iced Salad Bowl

1

3

Have ready two glass freezerproof bowls – one slightly larger than the other – room in the deep freezer to accommodate them and, finally, a little time to prepare this very attractive iced bowl – a novel way to serve shellfish.

Select some ingredients which will freeze in the 'bowl' – lemon and lime slices, nasturtium flowers or other edible petals, small shells and some fresh herbs.

Fill the larger of the two bowls with approximately 1 in/2.5 cm water. Use *boiled* water – this will give clearer ice. Add some fruit slices, herbs etc and freeze until solid.

To remove the smaller bowl, remove the weights, rub the inside of the bowl with a hot, damp cloth or fill it with warm water. Carefully loosen it and remove.

To remove the outer bowl, fill a sink with warm water and sit the bowl to just below its rim in the water for a minute or until it loosens. Do not allow it to begin melting.

Store in the freezer in a large plastic bag or use immediately, filled with cooked shellfish.

VARIATION Use just flower petals and the iced bowl is perfect for serving ice cream from.

2

Place the second bowl inside the large bowl. Position it centrally and weight it down (use some frozen food to do this). Pour approx 1 in/2.5 cm water between the two bowls, add some more garnishes and freeze again. Repeat the process until the ice bowl is complete, and well frozen.

Smoked Salmon Cornets

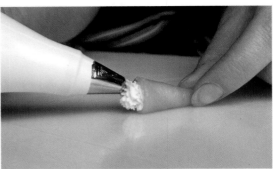

1

Cut some thin slices of smoked salmon into circles, using a 3½-in/9-cm diameter pastry cutter. Cut each circle into quarters.

2

Roll each quarter into a conical shape. Position three cornets on the plate and pipe a little cream cheese or savoury butter (see page 72) into their centres.

USE AS A
GARNISH FOR:

FISH DISHES

SEAFOOD,
AVOCADO OR
CUCUMBER HORS
D'OEUVRES, PÂTÉS
AND MOUSSES

EGG DISHES

OR SERVE ON A
SMALL SQUARE OF
BREAD OR A
CROÛTE (SEE PAGE
58) AS A CANAPÉ.

3

Top the piped cream with a little lumpfish roe or caviar and, finally, tuck a sprig or two of fresh dill, fennel or another delicate herb around the base of the cornets.

4

VARIATION The cornets can also be arranged on Grooved Lemon Slices (see page 15).

Miniature Kebabs

1

2

Select a variety of small and colourful food such as bacon rolls, baby sweetcorn (sliced), button mushrooms, prawns, red and yellow peppers, cherry tomatoes, cubes of ham, pineapple and apricots and thin slices of stem ginger.

Cook the vegetables until *al dente*. Refresh in cold water and drain thoroughly. Cut the selected fruits, meats and vegetables into even-sized, attractive pieces.

Thread onto wooden cocktail sticks or short wooden skewers (maximum 4 in/10 cm in length). Brush liberally with melted butter or oil and cook under a preheated grill, turning frequently with tongs, until cooked. The cooking time will vary according to the types of food used.

USE AS A
GARNISH FOR:

EGG AND CHEESE
DISHES

ROAST AND
GRILLED (BROILED)
MEATS

POULTRY

FISH

SAVOURY PANCAKES
(CRÊPES) AND
OMELETTES

RICE AND PASTA
DISHES

OR SERVE AS AN
APPETIZER

3

Serve immediately, topped with fresh sprigs of herbs.

NOTE Select the foods that will most enhance and complement your chosen main dish, such as pineapple, sweet peppers and stem ginger for pork, gammon and ham dishes, or bacon rolls, mushrooms and tomatoes for grilled poultry and meat dishes.

THE RECIPES

Cream of Carrot Soup (Crème de Crécy)

SERVES 4 TO 6

A warming soup, both in colour and taste. The rice acts as a thickening agent.

INGREDIENTS

2 tbsp/25 g/1 oz butter

2 medium onions, finely chopped

1½ lb/750 g/1½ lb carrots, peeled and grated

1 tbsp/15 ml/1 tbsp tomato purée (paste)

¼ cup/25 g/1 oz long grain rice

4½ cups/1 L/1¾ pts chicken stock (broth), ideally homemade

salt and freshly ground black pepper, to taste

6 tbsp/90 ml/6 tbsp double (heavy) cream

TO GARNISH:

Carrot Curls (see page 32)
fresh coriander (cilantro)
Croûtons (see page 58)

PREPARATION

● Melt the butter in a large saucepan. Stir in the onions and cook gently for 5 minutes, until softened, but not browned.

● Add the carrots, tomato purée, rice and 4 tbsp/60 ml/4 tbsp of stock. Cover tightly and 'sweat' the vegetables for a further 5–10 minutes. Pour in the remaining stock and simmer, uncovered, for 30 minutes.

● Liquidize the soup in batches – or pass through a fine sieve. Return to the rinsed pan. Season to taste. Stir in half of the cream and gently reheat *without boiling*.

● Serve garnished with a swirl of cream, one or two carrot curls, a sprinkling of freshly chopped coriander (cilantro) and accompany with some crunchy croûtons.

SUITABLE FOR FREEZING

Avocado Mousse

SERVES 4 TO 6

The delicate green of avocado makes this mousse an attractive starter to a meal, or a light summer lunch, either on its own or with prawns (shrimp). Try to make the mousse just a few hours in advance, to get the best of its colour.

INGREDIENTS

1 tbsp/15 ml/1 tbsp powdered gelatine (gelatin)

150 ml/¼ pt/⅔ cup chicken stock (broth), ideally homemade

2 medium avocado pears

juice of ½ small lemon

1 small shallot or 3 spring onions (scallions), white parts only

salt and freshly ground black pepper

dash Tabasco sauce

⅔ cup/150 ml/¼ pt mayonnaise

⅔ cup/150 ml/¼ pt double (heavy) cream

TO GARNISH:

Chilli Flowers (see page 33) OR
White Radish Flower (see page 44)
grooved cucumber slices

PREPARATION

● Sprinkle the gelatine over 3 tbsp/45 ml/3 tbsp of the stock in a small bowl. Place the bowl over a saucepan of simmering water and stir until dissolved.

● Stir in the remaining stock and leave to cool slightly.

● Halve the avocados, discard the stones and scoop out the flesh, scraping the shells well, as it is the flesh right next to the shell which gives the mousse its delicate green colour.

● In a food processor or blender, liquidize the flesh with the lemon juice and onion, until smooth. Add the seasoning and Tabasco sauce, and finally mix in the gelatine mixture. Stir well. Adjust the seasoning to taste. Cool.

● When the avocado mixture is just beginning to set, stir in the mayonnaise and cream. Pour into a well-oiled 4½-cup/1-litre/1¾-pt mould (or individual ramekins). Cover with cling film (plastic wrap) and chill until firm. To serve, ease the mousse from the mould onto a serving platter. (If the mousse is a little stubborn in unmoulding, wipe the outside of the mould with a hot, damp cloth.)

● Garnish with a border of grooved cucumber slices. Top with some Chilli Flowers or a White Radish Flower. Accompany with a Vinaigrette Dressing (see page 109), perhaps with some very finely chopped sweet red pepper stirred in, and plenty of crusty bread.

Fried Camembert with Cranberry Sauce

SERVES 4

The sharp flavour of the sauce ideally partners these cheese croquettes to make a colourful first course. The melted cheese oozes out to mingle with the sauce.

INGREDIENTS

1 round Camembert, weighing approx. ½ lb/225 g/8 oz

1 tbsp/15 ml/1 tbsp seasoned plain flour

1 egg, lightly beaten

1½ cups/75 g/3 oz fresh breadcrumbs

Oil for deep-fat frying

CRANBERRY SAUCE

1 cup/175 g/6 oz cranberries (fresh or frozen)

juice of 1 orange

2 tbsp/30 ml/2 tbsp ruby port or water

scant ½ cup/75 g/3 oz caster (superfine) sugar

TO GARNISH:

Orange Julienne (see page 22)
Frosted Cranberries (see page 29)
bay or mint leaves

PREPARATION

● Divide the Camembert into eight wedges and toss in the seasoned flour. Using two forks, dip the cheese in the egg and then in the breadcrumbs, to coat evenly. Repeat process if necessary. Chill the cheese 'croquettes' for 30 minutes.

● Meanwhile, make the sauce. Bring the cranberries, orange juice and port or water to the boil. Reduce heat, cover and simmer for 5 minutes.

● Stir in the sugar, and simmer for a further 5 minutes or until the cranberries are tender and the liquid is syrupy; keep warm.

● Deep fry the Camembert, four pieces at a time, at 350°F/180°C for 2 minutes or until golden. Drain well on absorbent kitchen paper (paper towel) and keep warm. Fry the remaining batch.

● Serve two hot cheese croquettes for each person, with some warm cranberry sauce. Garnish with a few strands of Orange Julienne and a small cluster of Frosted Cranberries grouped with a mint or bay leaf.

VARIATIONS: Redcurrant, gooseberry or plum sauce is equally delicious. Goats cheese or Brie can replace the Camembert.

Stilton Pears

SERVES 6

An interesting contrast in flavours – the sweet fruit and tangy sharp Stilton with a refreshing mint dressing.

INGREDIENTS

3 firm, ripe pears

heaped 1 cup/225 g/8 oz caster (superfine) sugar

1¼ cups/300 ml/½ pt water

1 tbsp/15 ml/1 tbsp lemon juice

1 egg

1 tbsp/15 ml/1 tbsp white wine vinegar

¾ cup/75 g/3 oz Stilton cheese, crumbled

⅔ cup/150 ml/¼ pt double (heavy) cream

1 tbsp/15 ml/1 tbsp chopped fresh mint

salt and freshly ground black pepper, to taste

TO GARNISH:

paprika for dusting
4 Tomato Roses (see page 41)
fresh mint leaves

PREPARATION

● Peel, halve and core the pears. Dissolve the sugar in the water and lemon juice over a low heat, then boil for 2–3 minutes. Gently poach the pears in the syrup until tender. Time will vary, depending upon the ripeness of the fruit. Cool.

● To make the dressing, break the egg into a glass bowl and beat with a whisk. Add the wine vinegar and 1 tbsp/15 ml/1 tbsp of the pear syrup.

● Stand the bowl over a pan of simmering water and stir the egg mixture steadily until it begins to thicken. Add the Stilton cheese and continue stirring until the cheese has melted and the dressing is smooth and thickened. Season lightly and leave to cool.

● Lightly whip the cream and fold into the dressing together with the chopped mint. Divide the dressing between six small plates and evenly coat each plate.

● Place a pear half on each serving plate. Slice it from its wide base to the stalk end, taking care not to cut right the way through. Gently fan the slices out. Lightly dust the pear fan with paprika, and garnish the pear with a Tomato Rose and two or three mint leaves.

● Serve with melba toast.

VARIATIONS: Try Roquefort cheese or another type of blue-veined cheese instead of the Stilton. Canned pear halves could be used instead of fresh, but choose a brand in natural juice, not syrup.

Smoked Trout Mousse

Marinated Kipper Fillets

Smoked Trout Mousse

A light fish mousse—simple to make and delightful to serve as a starter or light lunch.

INGREDIENTS

4 fresh smoked trout (each weighing approx. 6 oz/175 g/6 oz), skinned, boned and flaked

2 tbsp/30 ml/2 tbsp lemon juice

⅔ cup/150 ml/¼ pt mayonnaise

⅔ cup/150 ml/¼ pt double (heavy) cream, lightly whipped

2 tsp/10 ml/2 tsp creamed horseradish sauce

cayenne pepper

salt

1 tbsp/15 ml/1 tbsp powdered gelatine (gelatin)

2 egg whites

TO GARNISH:

chopped aspic (see page 76)
6 Choux Pastry Swans (see page 63)
12 Smoked Salmon Cornets (see page 82)
6 Lemon Twists (see page 16)
6 sprigs fresh dill

PREPARATION

● Sprinkle the trout with the lemon juice. In a food processor or liquidizer, process the trout together with the mayonnaise, cream and horseradish sauce, until smooth. Season with cayenne pepper and salt.

● Sprinkle the gelatine over 6 tbsp/90 ml/6 tbsp water in a small bowl. Stand the bowl over a pan of boiling water until the gelatine has dissolved. Allow to cool slightly before stirring into the trout purée.

● Beat the egg whites until they form soft peaks. Gently fold them into the trout purée. Divide the mixture between six small ramekin dishes. Level the surface. Chill for at least 2 hours.

● Turn the trout ramekins out onto individual serving plates. Place the chopped aspic and a Lemon Twist alongside each mousse and 'float' a Choux Pastry Swan on the aspic. Place two Smoked Salmon Cornets and a sprig of fresh dill on top of the mousse.

● Accompany with thin slices of wholemeal bread and butter or melba toast.

VARIATIONS: Try poached salmon or smoked haddock for a change.

SUITABLE FOR FREEZING

Marinated Kipper Fillets

After the kipper fillets have had several days marinating, you will have your guests guessing what this declicious fish is. Have a good supply of crusty bread to mop up the juices.

INGREDIENTS

¾ lb/375 g/12 oz kipper fillets (approx. 8 fillets), or other smoked fish fillets

1 medium onion, thinly sliced

2 tsp/10 ml/2 tsp coriander seeds, crushed

2 bay leaves

freshly ground black pepper

¾ cup/175 ml/6 fl oz sunflower oil

4 tbsp/60 ml/4 tbsp red wine vinegar

1 tbsp/15 ml/1 tbsp soft brown sugar

grated rind of 1 lemon

2 tsp/10 ml/2 tsp mustard powder

TO GARNISH:

Grooved Lemon Slices (see page 15)
Spring Onion (Scallion) Flowers (see page 38)
fresh coriander

PREPARATION

● Using a sharp knife, remove the skins from the kippers. Slice the kipper fillets diagonally into long strips. Layer in a shallow, wide dish, together with the onion, crushed coriander seeds, bay leaves and black pepper.

● In a screw top jar, shake together the oil, vinegar, brown sugar, lemon rind and mustard powder until well blended and dissolved.

● Pour the dressing over the kipper fillets. Cover tightly with cling film (plastic wrap) and refrigerate for 2–5 days (the longer the better). Turn the fillets occasionally in the marinade.

● Serve the kipper fillets, surrounded by Grooved Lemon Slices and topped with sprigs of fresh coriander and a Spring Onion (Scallion) Flower.

Cucumber & Cream Cheese Mousse

SERVES 6 TO 8 AS A FIRST COURSE, 4 AS A LIGHT LUNCH

A light, refreshing start to a meal, or a delicious summer lunch!

INGREDIENTS

1 large cucumber, peeled

salt

¾ cup/175 g/6 oz cream cheese

1 tsp/5 ml/1 tsp finely chopped shallot or spring onion (scallion)

freshly ground black pepper

⅔ cup/150 ml/¼ pt hot vegetable stock (broth)

1 tbsp/15 ml/1 tbsp powdered gelatine (gelatin) soaked in 3 tbsp/45 ml/3 tbsp water

2 tbsp/30 ml/2 tbsp white wine vinegar

1 tbsp/15 ml/1 tbsp caster (superfine) sugar

pinch ground mace

⅔ cup/150 ml/¼ pt double (heavy) cream, lightly whipped

TO GARNISH:

Star Fruit (Carambola) (see page 30)
Feathery Cucumber Fans (see page 34)

PREPARATION

● Dice the cucumber finely and liberally sprinkle with salt. Leave pressed between two plates for 30 minutes.

● Cream the cheese together with the chopped shallot and salt and pepper.

● Pour the hot stock onto the soaked gelatine and stir, until the gelatine has dissolved. Blend into the cream cheese.

● Drain the cucumber. Rinse, then dry thoroughly with absorbent kitchen paper (paper towel). Mix the cucumber with the wine vinegar, sugar and mace.

● When the cream cheese mixture is cold and starting to set, fold in the cucumber and the lightly whipped cream. Divide between six to eight lightly oiled ramekins and chill for a couple of hours. Remove from the refrigerator half an hour before serving.

● To serve, unmould the mousse. Spoon over a little vinaigrette dressing (see page 109), if desired, and garnish with Star Fruit (Carambola) and Feathery Cucumber Fans.

VARIATION: If to be served as part of a buffet or a light lunch, a lightly greased 4½ cup/1 litre/1¾ pt ring mould can be used instead of the ramekin dishes, and the centre filled with watercress, nasturtium flowers or frisée lettuce.

Chinese Vegetable Salad

SERVES 4

A crisp, refreshing salad that makes a cooling accompaniment to sizzling meat or spare ribs.

INGREDIENTS

8 large radishes

2 large carrots, peeled

4 sticks celery

8 spring onions (scallions), trimmed

DRESSING

¼ cup/45 ml/ 3 tbsp olive oil

1 tbsp/15 ml/1 tbsp lemon juice

1 tsp/5 ml/1 tsp light soy sauce

1 tsp/5 ml/1 tsp caster (superfine) sugar

freshly ground black pepper

PREPARATION

● Following the instructions on page 35, make eight Radish Marguerites. Drop into a bowl of iced water.

● Slice the carrots, lengthwise, thinly, and then into long, narrow strips. Add to the water.

● Following the instructions on page 54, prepare the celery julienne-style, but do not blanch. Add to the water.

● Prepare the Spring Onion (Scallion) Curls by following the instructions on page 39. Add to the water.

● Leave all the vegetables to soak for 2 hours.

● Put the dressing ingredients into a screw-top jar and shake vigorously to form an emulsion.

● Drain and dry the vegetables, toss in the dressing and serve immediately.

VARIATIONS: Try adding other vegetables, such as baby sweetcorn, water chestnuts or mange tout (snow peas). This could be served on a bed of lettuce leaves.

Beetroot & Lime Jelly Salad

SERVES 4 TO 6

This is one of the simplest, and most successful, vegetable salad dishes that always looks impressive yet couldn't be easier. It is delicious with cold meats.

INGREDIENTS

one 2½-cup/600-ml/1-pt lime jelly tablet

3 tbsp/45 ml/3 tbsp white wine vinegar

1½ lb/750 g/1½ lb young beetroot (beets), cooked and peeled

4 spring onions (scallions), trimmed and finely chopped

freshly ground black pepper

TO GARNISH:

Curly Tops (see page 49)
lime julienne (see page 23)

PREPARATION

● Make up the lime jelly following the instructions on the packet. Stir in the white wine vinegar.

● Roughly chop the beetroot and put in a bowl, together with the finely chopped spring onions (scallions) and some freshly ground black pepper. When the jelly has cooled slightly, pour over the beetroot and leave until firmly set.

● With a small, sharp knife, chop the jelly and beetroot into small pieces. Spoon out onto a serving dish and garnish with Curly Tops from baby beetroot and a sprinkling of lime julienne.

VARIATION: Raspberry jelly tastes equally good in this recipe, but does not offer the lime's sharp contrast in flavour.

Cracked Wheat Salad

SERVES 4 TO 6

Once the flavours have had time to develop, this salad is irresistable on its own as well as an accompaniment to cold meats and fish dishes. You can use the chicory (endive) leaves to scoop up the salad.

INGREDIENTS

1 cup/200 g/7 oz cracked wheat or burghul

4 large spring onions (scallions)

1⅓ cups/75 g/3 oz flat-leaf parsley

2 tbsp/30 ml/2 tbsp fresh mint

¼ cup/60 ml/4 tbsp olive oil

¼ cup/60 ml/4 tbsp fresh lemon juice

salt, to taste

TO GARNISH:

4–6 Tomato Crabs (see page 40)
2 chicory (endive) heads, separated into leaves
8–12 Chilli Flowers (see page 33)
flat-leaf parsley or mint sprigs

PREPARATION

● Soak the cracked wheat or burghul in cold water for 20 minutes. Drain well, and squeeze out excess water with your hands.

● Finely chop the spring onions (scallions), parsley and mint, and combine with the cracked wheat in a large bowl. Sprinkle in the olive oil, lemon juice and salt and mix thoroughly.

● Taste and adjust the seasoning. Cover and chill for 2–3 hours to allow the flavours to mingle.

● Spoon the salad onto individual side plates and garnish each with some chicory leaves, a Tomato Crab, two Chilli Flowers, and sprigs of flat-leaf parsley or mint.

Warm Pigeon Salad

SERVES 4

This salad is relatively quick and simple to prepare, and makes a little pigeon go a long way! The crunchy nuts, croûtons and bacon rolls provide a delicious contrast.

INGREDIENTS

3 pigeons, each weighing approx. ¾ lb/375 g/12 oz

2 tbsp/25 g/1 oz butter

1 tsp/5 ml/1 tsp Dijon mustard

1 clove garlic, crushed (minced)

3 tbsp/45 ml/3 tbsp red wine vinegar

1 cup/90 ml/6 tbsp walnut or olive oil

salt and freshly ground black pepper

1 head curly endive (chicory)

2 tomatoes

TO GARNISH:

12 Bacon Rolls (see page 79)
Croûtons (see page 58)
½ cup/50 g/2 oz walnut halves

Oven temperature: 425°F/220°C/Gas 7

PREPARATION

● Preheat the oven. Smear the pigeons with the butter, then roast with the Bacon Rolls for 20 minutes.

● While the pigeons are cooking, make the dressing. Put the mustard, garlic and wine vinegar into a bowl. Gradually beat in the walnut or olive oil. Season to taste.

● Wash the curly endive and break each leaf into pieces. Skin and seed the tomatoes, then cut the flesh into neat strips.

● Remove the pigeons and bacon rolls. Switch off oven, and put the Croûtons into the oven to just warm through. Cut the pigeon breasts into fine slices.

● Toss the endive in a little of the dressing. Divide between four plates. Arrange the pigeon slices on top and then scatter over the strips of tomato.

● Garnish with the Bacon Rolls, walnut halves and the warm Croûtons. Spoon over the remaining dressing, and serve while the pigeon is still warm.

VARIATIONS: Smoked chicken or duck make excellent substitutes for the pigeon.

Russian Chicken & Potato Salad

SERVES 4

A satisfying meal in itself, this is perfect with a mixed green salad for a summer picnic.

INGREDIENTS

1 lb/500 g/1 lb cooked boneless chicken breasts (fillets)

½ lb/225 g/8 oz potatoes, boiled in their skins

2 large gherkins (dill pickles)

2 tsp/10 ml/2 tsp Worcestershire sauce

⅔ cup/150 ml/¼ pt mayonnaise

1⅔ cups/200 g/7 oz button mushrooms, halved

4 black olives, stoned and halved

salt and freshly ground black pepper

TO GARNISH:

4 hard-boiled eggs, sliced
strips of red pimento (canned)
stuffed green olives, sliced
chopped fresh parsley

PREPARATION

● Skin the chicken and cut the meat into thin strips.

● Peel the potatoes and cut into even sized strips.

● Cut the gherkins (dill pickles) into julienne strips.

● Beat the Worcestershire sauce into the mayonnaise. Then carefully fold in the chicken, potatoes, gherkins and mushrooms and olives. Season to taste.

● Pile the salad onto a shallow serving dish and surround with the egg slices. Arrange fine strips of pimento and olive slices over the top and sprinkle with the freshly chopped parsley.

Chicken, Cheese & Chive Terrine

SERVES 8

INGREDIENTS

¾ lb/375 g/2 oz boneless chicken breast (fillet)

6 tbsp/60 ml/6 tbsp brandy

1 clove garlic, crushed (minced)

1 tbsp/15 ml/1 tbsp chopped fresh parsley

¾ lb/375 g/12 oz boneless chicken thighs

1½ lb/750 g/1½ lb stewing pork

8 rashers (strips) fatty bacon

scant 1 cup/200 g/7 oz cream cheese

½ cup/125 ml/4 fl oz double (heavy) cream

2 eggs

grated rind of ½ lemon

1 tbsp/15 ml/1 tbsp chopped fresh chives

salt and freshly ground black pepper

TO GARNISH:

aspic glaze (see page 76)
chive stems
red pepper and egg decorations (see pages 36 and 67)
Spring Onion (Scallion) Flowers (see page 38)

Oven temperature: 400°F/200°C/Gas 6

PREPARATION

● Marinate the chicken breasts in the brandy, garlic and half the parsley for 2 hours.

● Preheat the oven. Mince (grind) the chicken thighs, pork and bacon together. Blend with the cream cheese, cream, beaten eggs and lemon rind. Add the parsley, chives and the marinade drained from the chicken. Season well.

● Put a third of the chicken forcemeat into a lightly oiled 8¾-cup/2-litre/3½-pt loaf tin or terrine dish. Top with half the chicken breasts, then another layer of forcemeat, then the rest of the chicken breasts and, finally, the remaining forcemeat.

● Cover and bake in a roasting pan of water for approximately 1½–2 hours.

● Cool, then press with a weight and refrigerate for at least one day.

● To garnish, invert the terrine onto a wire cooling rack. Spoon over some cool, halfset aspic jelly to form a glaze. Decorate the surface of the terrine with chive stems, red pepper and egg shapes, and then coat with another layer of aspic. Surround the base of the terrine with salad. Serve with some Spring Onion (Scallion) Flowers.

Crab Flan

SERVES 6 TO 8

This eye-catching flan makes a little crab go a long way. This is a perfect dish for a lunchtime treat, accompanied with new potatoes and a tomato salad.

INGREDIENTS

1 medium cucumber

salt and freshly ground black pepper

1 cup/185 g/6 oz fresh dark crabmeat

⅔ cup/150 ml/¼ pt Béchamel Sauce (see page 108)

¼ cup/50 g/2 oz butter, softened

1–2 tbsp/15–30 ml/1–2 tbsp double (heavy) cream, lightly whipped

⅔ cup/150 ml/¼ pt mayonnaise

1 cup/185 g/6 oz fresh light crabmeat

one × 9-in/23-cm cooked pastry case

TO GARNISH:

2 eggs, hardboiled
chopped fresh parsley

PREPARATION

● Peel and finely slice the cucumber. Sprinkle the slices liberally with salt and leave the slices pressed between two plates for 30 minutes. Drain, rinse with iced water, then dry the cucumber slices and season with pepper.

● Work the dark crabmeat into the cold Béchamel Sauce. Blend in the softened butter and the cream. Season to taste.

● Blend the mayonnaise with the white crabmeat. Season to taste.

● Spread the dark crabmeat mixture over the base of the pastry case, then evenly scatter the cucumber slices on top and, finally, spread over the white crabmeat. Chill.

● Garnish the flan with the sieved egg yolk, chopped egg white and parsley, as shown on page 66.

Stir-Fried Beef with Ginger

Baked Fish with Lime and Herb Butter

Stir-fried Beef with Ginger

SERVES 3 TO 4

This is such an adaptable recipe – the meat and vegetable can be varied to suit availability. Stir-fried dishes are easy, and quick, bringing out the natural flavours of fresh, lightly cooked vegetables. The meat really benefits from its marinating.

INGREDIENTS

¾ lb/375 g/12 oz lean beef steak (fillet is best)

2 cloves garlic

1-in/2.5-cm piece fresh root ginger, peeled

⅓ cup/90 ml/6 tbsp soya sauce

¼ cup/60 ml/4 tbsp dry sherry

1 tsp/5 ml/1 tsp cornflour (cornstarch)

1⅓ cup/225 g/8 oz (prepared weight) mixed vegetables (baby sweetcorn, mange tout (snow peas), sweet red pepper, spring onion (scallion), Chinese mushrooms, etc), cut into even-shaped slices or strips where necessary

2 tbsp/30 ml/2 tbsp groundnut oil

TO GARNISH:

Spring Onion (Scallion) Curls (see page 39)

PREPARATION

● Trim any fat off the meat and then cut into thin slices, across the grain. Arrange in a layer in a shallow dish.

● Finely chop the garlic and the ginger. Reserve half the ginger and sprinkle the rest, together with garlic, over the steak. Add the soya sauce and sherry. Cover and leave to marinate in the refrigerator for 10–12 hours or overnight, stirring at least once.

● Strain the meat (reserving the marinade) and toss in the cornflour (cornstarch). Heat a wok or large frying pan until hot. Add 1 tbsp/15 ml/1 tbsp of the oil and when it is just beginning to smoke, add the beef. Stir fry for 2 minutes, remove and keep warm.

● Wipe the pan clean with kitchen paper (paper towel) and add the remaining oil. When hot, stir fry the remaining ginger and the prepared vegetables for 2 minutes.

● Add 2 tbsp/30 ml/2 tbsp of the reserved marinade and 2 tbsp/30 ml/2 tbsp hot water. Return the meat to the pan and give the mixture a quick stir.

● Turn out onto a hot plate, and serve immediately, garnished with Spring Onion (Scallion) Curls and accompanied with plain boiled rice.

Baked Fish with Lime & Herb Butter

SERVES 4

The subtle flavours of fennel and lime blend beautifully with red mullet, snapper or rainbow trout.

INGREDIENTS

¼ cup/50 g/2 oz butter

4 medium fish or 1 large, cleaned

1 tsp/5 ml/1 tsp fennel seeds

2 limes

1¼ cups/300 ml/½ pt medium–sweet red wine

salt and freshly ground black pepper

TO GARNISH:

4 Lime Baskets (see page 20)
Fresh Herb Butter (see page 72)
Parisienne Potato Balls (see page 53)

Oven Temperature: 400°F/200°C/Gas 6

PREPARATION

● Preheat the oven. Lightly butter a shallow ovenproof dish. Place the fish in the bottom. Dot with the remaining butter and sprinkle with the fennel seeds.

● Using a vegetable peeler, cut several strips of the lime rind and put among the fish. Squeeze over the juice of the limes and pour the wine over the fish.

● Season well with salt and freshly ground black pepper. Cover tightly with foil and bake for about 25 minutes, or until the fish is cooked through and flakes easily when tested with the tip of a knife.

● Serve the fish with some of its juices, topped with a slice of Fresh Herb Butter (either fennel or parsley). Garnish each with a Lime Basket, some Parisienne Potato Balls and a few sprigs of fennel or dill.

VARIATION: Instead of the limes and wine, try orange and vermouth.

Spicy Lamb Kebabs

SERVES 4

A subtle flavour of the Middle East, conjured up in no time at all. These kebabs can even be made a day or two in advance, taking the heat out of preparing an informal supper party, perhaps.

INGREDIENTS

¼ cup/60 ml/4 tbsp Greek or natural (plain) yogurt

2 tbsp/30 ml/2 tbsp lemon juice

2 tbsp/30 ml/2 tbsp vegetable oil

1-in/2.5-cm piece fresh ginger, peeled and grated

1 clove garlic, crushed

1 tsp/5 ml/1 tsp ground cumin

½ tsp/2.5 ml/½ tsp ground coriander

¼ tsp grated nutmeg

¼ tsp ground cinnamon

1 tsp/5 ml/1 tsp salt

1½ lb/750 g/1½ lb lean lamb, cut into 1-in/2.5-cm cubes

TO GARNISH:

1 tbsp/15 g/½ oz toasted flaked almonds (see page 78)
fresh coriander sprigs
4 Lemon and Lime Twists (see page 16)
4 Poppadom Baskets (see page 59)

PREPARATION

● In a large bowl, thoroughly mix together the first 10 ingredients. Fold in the cubes of lamb, coating them well with the spicy marinade. Cover and refrigerate for 6–12 hours (or overnight), turning occasionally.

● Drain the meat, reserving the marinade, then thread onto four metal or wooden skewers. Cook under a preheated grill for 15–20 minutes or until done. (Baste with the remaining marinade and turn the kebabs frequently to cook them evenly.)

● Serve the kebabs on a bed of saffron rice. Sprinkle the toasted flaked almonds over the kebabs, and garnish each with a sprig of fresh coriander, a Lemon and Lime Twist and a crispy Poppadom Basket filled with diced tomato, cucumber and onion.

Wiener Schnitzel

SERVES 4

Wiener Schnitzel (or *Escalopes Viennoises*) is an Austrian speciality, simply prepared and garnished in the traditional way. Pork works equally well, if good veal is difficult to obtain.

INGREDIENTS

4 thin escalopes veal (or pork), each weighing approx. ¼ lb/125 g/4 oz

seasoned plain flour

1 egg, beaten

dried breadcrumbs

1 tbsp/15 ml/1 tbsp vegetable oil

¼ cup/50 g/2 oz butter

1 tbsp/15 ml/1 tbsp lemon juice

TO GARNISH:

4 Grooved Lemon Slices (see page 15)
4 anchovy fillets
4 tsp/20 ml/4 tsp capers, chopped
finely chopped fresh parsley
4 Lemon Pouches (see page 19)

PREPARATION

● Beat the escalopes between two pieces of greaseproof (waxed) paper or cling film (plastic film) until very thin. Dust with lightly seasoned flour. Dip in the beaten egg, and then in the breadcrumbs – shaking off any excess.

● Heat the oil and butter in a large frying pan. Fry the better side of the escalopes first, until golden brown, then turn over and brown the second side. Reduce the heat and cook for a further 3–4 minutes. Transfer the escalopes to a hot serving dish.

● Add the lemon juice to the juices in the pan. Strain around the veal.

● Top each escalope with a Grooved Lemon Slice, an anchovy fillet and some chopped capers. Sprinkle with parsley. Accompany with the Lemon Pouches, to be squeezed over the escalopes to release their juice.

Loin of Pork Normandy

SERVES 4

Any recipe which mentions 'Normandy' in its title usually includes in its list of ingredients fresh cream, crisp apples and the tiniest hint of Calvados! This recipe is no exception – the combined flavour of the succulent pork and a creamy apple sauce is irresistible.

INGREDIENTS

1 tbsp/15 ml/1 tbsp vegetable oil

1 tbsp/15 ml/1 tbsp butter

1½ lb/750 g/1½ lb boned loin of pork, rolled and tied

2 medium onions

2 crisp dessert apples, peeled, cored and sliced

3 tbsp/45 ml/3 tbsp Calvados

1 tbsp/15 ml/1 tbsp plain flour

1½ cups/375 ml/12 fl oz chicken stock (broth)

½ cup/125 ml/4 fl oz double (heavy) cream

salt and freshly ground black pepper

TO GARNISH:

Poached Apple (see page 27)
Julienne Bundles (see page 54)
watercress or sage leaves

Oven temperature: 350°F/180°C/Gas 4

PREPARATION

● Preheat the oven. Heat together the oil and butter in an ovenproof casserole. Seal the pork until golden brown all over, then transfer to a plate.

● Finely chop the onions and gently soften in the hot fat; stir in the apples and cook together for 5 minutes, until golden.

● Return the pork to the casserole and flambé with the Calvados. The simplest way to do this is to warm the spirit in a large ladle, ignite it, then pour it carefully over the pork. Allow the flames to die down, by which time the harshness of the alcohol will have evaporated, leaving a wonderful flavour.

● Stir the flour into the juices. Gradually add the stock and seasoning. Cover and cook for 1½–2 hours.

● To serve, remove the pork, slice, and keep warm. Strain the juices from the casserole into a small pan. Reduce, if necessary, over a high heat before stirring in the cream. Heat through gently for a few minutes. Adjust the seasoning to taste.

● Spoon the sauce over the pork slices. Garnish with Poached Apples, Julienne Bundles, and a sprig of watercress or fresh sage leaves.

Orange & Tarragon Chicken

SERVES 4

Tarragon is a classic partner for chicken and a perfect blend in flavour with this delicious orange-scented casserole.

INGREDIENTS

25 g/1 oz/2 tbsp butter

2 tbsp/30 ml/2 tbsp vegetable oil

4 boneless chicken breasts, each weighing approx. 6 oz/175 g/6 oz

1 large onion, finely chopped

1 cup/250 ml/8 fl oz frozen concentrated orange juice

⅔ cup/150 ml/¼ pt chicken stock (broth)

4 sprigs fresh tarragon or 1 tbsp/15 ml/1 tbsp dried tarragon

1 tbsp/15 ml/1 tbsp cornflour (cornstarch)

⅔ cup/150 ml/¼ pt soured cream

TO GARNISH:

4 sprigs fresh tarragon
1 large orange, julienned and segmented (see pages 22 and 21)
8 Pastry Fleurons (see page 62)

PREPARATION

● Heat the butter and oil in a flameproof casserole. Brown the chicken thoroughly on all sides. Put to one side and remove and discard the skin.

● Cook the onion in the casserole for 2–3 minutes. Stir in the orange juice, stock cube, water and chopped tarragon. Bring to the boil and return the chicken to the casserole. Cover and reduce the heat to a gentle simmer. Cook for 1 hour or until the chicken is tender.

● Blend the cornflour with 2 tbsp/30 ml/2 tbsp water and stir into the casserole. Bring to the boil, stirring, until the sauce is smooth and thickened. Switch off the heat and stir in the soured cream. Leave to warm through for a few minutes.

● Transfer the chicken breasts onto individual hot dinner plates. Spoon the sauce over the chicken.

● Garnish the breasts with the Orange Julienne. Fan the Orange Segments alongside the sauce, and garnish with the sprigs of fresh tarragon. Finally, arrange two Pastry Fleurons on each plate and serve immediately.

SUITABLE FOR FREEZING

Mustard Glazed Noisettes of Lamb

SERVES 4

INGREDIENTS

8 noisettes of lamb, each weighing approx. 2 oz/50 g/2 oz

salt and freshly ground black pepper

8 ¼-in/5-mm slices day-old bread

1 tbsp/15 ml/1 tbsp vegetable oil

¼ cup/50 g/2 oz butter

1 clove garlic, chopped

2 tbsp/30 ml/2 tbsp coarse grain mustard

4 tsp/20 ml/4 tsp demerara (light brown) sugar

½ cup/125 ml/4 fl oz dry red wine

TO GARNISH:

Turned Mushrooms Caps (see page 51)
4 Courgette (Zucchini) Barges (see page 48)
4 mint sprigs

PREPARATION

● Preheat a grill (broiler) to a medium setting. Trim any excess fat from the noisettes and season.

● Using a plain pastry cutter a little larger than the noisettes, stamp out 8 round croûtes of bread (see page 58).

● Heat together the oil and 3 tbsp/45g/1½ oz of the butter in a frying pan. Add the garlic and sauté for a minute. Seal the noisettes of lamb in the foaming fat, cooking each side for a couple of minutes each. Remove.

● Gently fry the croûtes in the fat left in the pan until crisp and evenly browned. Drain on absorbent kitchen paper (paper towel) and keep warm. Lightly sauté the turned mushrooms prepared for the garnish. Keep warm.

● Mix together the coarse grain mustard and the sugar.

● Grill (broil) the noisettes on one side for 2 minutes. Spread the mustard mixture over the other side of the noisettes and cook for a further 2–3 minutes or until browned and well glazed. While the meat is cooking boil the vegetables for the garnish.

● Meanwhile, add the red wine and the remaining butter to the frying pan and cook, stirring, until reduced and syrupy. Season to taste.

● To serve, place two noisettes of lamb, each on a bread croûte, on the serving plates and spoon a little of the pan juices over the top of each noisette. Garnish each plate with a few Turned Mushroom Caps, a sprig of mint and a warm Courgette Barge filled with an assortment of tiny vegetables.

BASIC RECIPES

Béchamel Sauce

MAKES APPROXIMATELY 1¼ cups/300 ml/½ pt

INGREDIENTS

1¼ cups/300 ml/½ pt milk

---

1 small bay leaf

---

sprig of fresh thyme

½ small onion

---

1 blade mace

---

6 whole black peppercorns

---

2 tbsp/25 g/1 oz butter

¼ cup/25 g/1 oz plain flour

---

salt and ground white pepper

PREPARATION

● Put the milk in a pan with the bay leaf, thyme, onion, mace and peppercorns. Slowly bring to the boil, then remove from heat, cover and leave to infuse for 15–20 minutes.

● In another saucepan, melt the butter, stir in the flour and cook for 2–3 minutes to form a roux.

● Strain the milk through a fine sieve and gradually blend it into the roux. Bring to the boil, stirring constantly, then simmer for 2–3 minutes. Season to taste.

Choux Paste

MAKES APPROXIMATELY ½ lb/225 g/8 oz

This pastry is a French speciality – light, crisp and airy, and best eaten as freshly as possible. It should almost treble in size during cooking and, for successful results, don't peep in the oven while it's baking!

INGREDIENTS

½ cup/65 g/2½ oz strong plain flour

pinch salt

¼ cup/50 g/2 oz butter

⅔ cup/150 ml/¼ pt water

2 eggs, beaten

Oven temperature: 425°F/220°C/Gas 7

PREPARATION

● Preheat the oven. Sift the flour and salt onto a piece of greaseproof (waxed) paper.

● Put the butter and water in a saucepan over a moderate heat and stir until the butter has melted.

● Bring the mixture to the boil, switch off the heat, and tip the flour into the pan all at once. Stir quickly with a wooden spoon until the flour has absorbed all the liquid and forms into a clean ball.

● Beat in the eggs, a little at a time, until the paste is shiny and thick enough to hold its own shape.

● Pipe or spoon shapes, as required, onto a greased, damp baking sheet. Lightly glaze, if wished, with beaten egg and milk.

● Bake until well risen, crisp and golden. Pierce each bun, to let the steam escape, before cooling on a wire rack.

VARIATION: For sweet choux paste, replace the salt with 1 tsp/5 ml/1 tsp caster (superfine) sugar.

Vinaigrette Dressing

MAKES ¾ cup/175 ml/6 fl oz

INGREDIENTS

½ cup/125 ml/4 fl oz olive oil

4 tbsp/60 ml/4 tbsp red or white wine vinegar

1½ tsp/7½ ml/1½ tsp mustard powder

½ level tsp *each* salt, ground black pepper and sugar

PREPARATION

● Whisk all the ingredients together, or shake in a screw top jar, to form an emulsion.

VARIATIONS: Any of the following can be added to the basic dressing according to the salad ingredients.

● 1–2 garlic cloves, crushed (minced)
● 2 tbsp/30 ml/2 tbsp chopped fresh tarragon or chives
● 1 tsp/5 ml/1 tsp anchovy essence (for cold fish)
● 2 tbsp/30 ml/2 tbsp *each* chopped fresh parsley and onion

Types of food and suggested garnishes

This list aims to give you a quick reference of garnishes suitable for various food categories. Use them only as suggestions.

Soups

Citrus Julienne	22
Carrot and Cucumber Curls	32
Chiffonade	33
Green Laces	50
Cheese Profiteroles	57
Croûtons	58
Egg Royale	68
Egg Strands	69
Shredded Pancakes (Crêpes)	70
Herbs	77
Crunchy Bacon Bits	80
Iced Salad Bowl	81

Salads & Vegetables

Lime Basket	20
Citrus Segments	21
Citrus Julienne	22
Apple Peony	24
Kiwi Fans	25
Nutty Pineapple Slices	28
Star Fruit (Carambola)	30
Carrot & Cucumber Curls	32
Chilli Flowers	33
Feathery Cucumber Fans & Fleurs-de-Lys	34
Radish Bud & Marguerite	35
Green, Red & Yellow Peppers	36
Spring Onion (Scallion) Bows, Curls & Flowers	38–9
Tomato Crabs	40
Tomato Rose	41
Tomato Tulip	42
Onion Rings	43
Onion Chrysanthemum	43
White Radish Flower (daikon or mooli)	44
Asparagus Tips with Parma Ham	46
Deep-Fried Celery Leaves	47
Courgette (Zucchini) Barges	48
Curly Tops	49
Green Laces	50
Turned Mushroom Caps	51
Potato Baskets or Nests	52
Vegetable Coils	54
Croûtons	58
Poppadom Baskets	59
Chopped Egg Garnishes	66
Egg Flowers	67
Speciality Butters	72
Butter Balls	73

Butter Curls	74
Aspic	76
Herbs	77
Nuts	78
Crunchy Bacon Bits	80

Hors d'Oeuvres & Cânapés

Twisted Lemon Fans	17
Lemon in a Pouch	19
Lime Basket	20
Kiwi Fans	25
Melon 'Grapes'	26
Carrot & Cucumber Curls	34
Cucumber Fleurs-de-Lys	34
Radish Bud & Marguerite	35
Green, Red & Yellow Peppers	36
Spring Onion (Scallion) Bows, Curls & Flowers	38–9
Tomato Crabs	40
Tomato Rose	41
Tomato Tulip	42
White Radish Flower (daikon or mooli)	44
Asparagus Tips with Parma Ham	46
Courgette (Zucchini) Barges	48
Curly Tops	49
Choux Pastry Swans	63
Chopped Egg Garnish	66
Egg Flowers	67
Aspic	76
Herbs	77
Nuts	78
Bacon Rolls	79
Smoked Salmon Cornets	82
Miniature Kebabs	83

Pasta, Rice & Potatoes

Lemon Half With a Knot	14
Carrot & Cucumber Curls	32
Chilli Flowers	33
Feathery Cucumber Fans & Fleurs-de-lys	34
Green, Red & Yellow Peppers	36
Spring Onion (Scallion) Bows, Curls & Flowers	38–9
Tomato Crabs	40
Tomato Rose	41

Tomato Tulip	42
Turned Mushroom Caps	51
Potato Allumettes	51
Potato Baskets or Nests	52
Parisienne Potatoes	53
Julienne Bundles	54
Speciality Butters	72
Butter Balls	73
Butter Curls	74
Herbs	77
Crunchy Bacon Bits	80
Miniature Kebabs	83

Cheese & Egg Dishes

Poached Pears	27
Green, Red & Yellow Peppers	36
Gherkin (Dill Pickle) Fans	38
Spring Onion (Scallion) Bows, Curls & Flowers	38–9
Tomato Crabs	40
Tomato Rose	41
Tomato Tulip	42
Onion Rings	43
Onion Chrysanthemum	43
Asparagus Tips with Parma Ham	46
Deep-Fried Celery Leaves	47
Courgette (Zucchini) Barges	48
Green Laces	50
Turned Mushroom Caps	51
Julienne Bundles	54
Crispy Bread Cases	58
Pastry Horns	61
Chopped Egg Garnishes	66
Egg Flowers	67
Aspic	76
Herbs	77
Nuts	78
Bacon Rolls	79
Crunchy Bacon Bits	80
Smoked Salmon Cornets	82
Miniature Kebabs	83

Pâtés, Terrines & Mousses

Grooved Lemon Slices	15
Citrus Twists, Butterflies & Swans	16–18
Twisted Lemon Fans	19

Lime Basket	20
Citrus Segments	21
Apple Peony	24
Kiwi Fans	25
Melon 'Grapes'	26
Frosted Cranberries	29
Star Fruit (Carambola)	30
Carrot & Cucumber Curls	32
Chilli Flowers	33
Feathery Cucumber Fans & Fleurs-de-lys	34
Radish Bud & Marguerite	35
Green, Red & Yellow Peppers	36
Gherkin (Dill Pickle) Fans	38
Spring Onion (Scallion) Bows, Curls & Flowers	38–9
Tomato Crabs	40
Tomato Rose	41
Tomato Tulip	42
Onion Rings	43
Onion Chrysanthemum	43
White Radish Flower (daikon or mooli)	44
Asparagus Tips with Parma Ham	46
Curly Tops	49
Turned Mushroom Caps	51
Choux Pastry Swan	63
Chopped Egg Garnishes	66
Egg Flowers	67
Aspic	76
Herbs	77
Nuts	78
Smoked Salmon Cornets	82

Pastry & Savoury Flans

Grooved Lemon Slices	15
Citrus Twists, Butterflies & Swans	16–18
Feathery Cucumber Fans	34
Green, Red & Yellow Peppers	36
Spring Onion (Scallion) Bows, Curls & Flowers	38–9
Pastry Garnishes for Pies	60
Pastry Fleurons	60
Pastry Horns	64
Chopped Egg Garnishes	66
Egg Flowers	67
Aspic	76
Herbs	77
Bacon Rolls	79
Smoked Salmon Cornets	82

Fish & Shellfish

Lemon Half with a Knot	14
Grooved Lemon Slices	15
Citrus Twists, Butterflies & Swans	16–18
Twisted Lemon Fans	17
Lemon in a Pouch	18
Lime Basket	20
Citrus Segments	21
Citrus Julienne	22
Apple Peony	24
Kiwi Fans	25
Melon 'Grapes'	26
Carrot & Cucumber Curls	32
Feathery Cucumber Fans & Fleurs-de-lys	34
Tomato Crabs	40
Tomato Rose	41
Tomato Tulip	42
Asparagus Tips with Parma Ham	46
Deep-Fried Celery Leaves	47
Courgette (Zucchini) Barges	48
Potato Allumettes	51
Potato Baskets or Nests	52
Parisienne Potato Balls	53
Julienne Bundles	54
Pastry Fleurons	62
Choux Pastry Swans	63
Pastry Horns	64
Chopped Egg Garnishes	66
Speciality Butters	72
Butter Balls	73
Aspic	76
Herbs	77
Nuts	78
Crunchy Bacon Bits (with haddock)	80
Iced Salad Bowl	81
Smoked Salmon Cornets	82
Miniature Kebabs	83

Meat

Lemon Half with a Knot	14
Grooved Lemon Slices	15
Lemon in a Pouch	19
Lime Basket	20
Citrus Segments	21
Orange Jelly Wedges	21
Citrus Julienne	22
Apple Peony	24
Kiwi Fans	25

Melon 'Grapes'	26
Poached Pears	27
Nutty Pineapple Slices	28
Frosted Cranberries	29
Star Fruit (Carambola)	30
Chilli Flowers	33
Feathery Cucumber Fans & Fleurs-de-Lys	34
Radish Bud & Marguerite	35
Green, Red & Yellow Peppers	36
Gherkin (Dill Pickle) Fans	38
Spring Onion (Scallion) Bows, Curls & Flowers	38–9
Tomato Crabs	40
Tomato Rose	41
Tomato Tulip	42
Onion Rings	43
Onion Chrysanthemum	43
White Radish Flower (mooli or daikon)	44
Asparagus Tips with Parma Ham	45
Deep-Fried Celery Leaves	47
Courgette (Zucchini) Barges	48
Green Laces	50
Turned Mushroom Caps	51
Potato Allumettes	51
Parisienne Potato Balls	53
Julienne Bundles	54
Vegetable Coils	54
Crispy Bacon Cases	56
Croûtes	58
Pastry Fleurons	62
Pastry Horns	64
Speciality Butters	72
Aspic	76
Herbs	77
Nuts	78
Miniature Kebabs	83

Poultry & Game

Lemon Half with a Knot	14
Twisted Lemon Fans	17
Lemon in a Pouch	19
Citrus Segments	21
Orange Jelly Wedges	21
Citrus Julienne	22
Kiwi Fans	25
Melon 'Grapes'	26
Poached Pears	27
Nutty Pineapple Slices	28
Frosted Cranberries	29

Star Fruit (Carambola)	30
Chilli Flowers	33
Tomato Crabs	40
Tomato Rose	41
Tomato Tulip	42
Onion Rings	43
Courgette (Zucchini) Barges	48
Green Laces	50
Turned Mushroom Caps	51
Potato Allumettes	51
Potato Baskets or Nests	52
Parisienne Potato Balls	53
Julienne Bundles	54
Crispy Bread Cases	56
Golden Breadcrumbs	57
Croûtes	58
Pastry Fleurons	62
Pastry Horns	64
Aspic	76
Herbs	77
Nuts	78
Bacon Rolls	79
Miniature Kebabs	83

Oriental, Eastern & Spicy Dishes

Citrus Julienne	28
Chilli Flowers	33
Radish Bud & Marguerite	35
Green, Red & Yellow Peppers	36
Spring Onion (Scallion) Curls, Bows & Flowers	38–9
Tomato Tulip	42
White Radish Flower (daikon or mooli)	44
Poppadom Baskets	59
Herbs	77
Nuts	78

Drinks and Punches

Grooved Lemon Slices	15
Herbs	77

Cheese Boards

Lemon Half with a Knot	14
Melon 'Grapes'	26
Frosted Cranberries	29
Tomato Crabs	40
Tomato Rose	41
Tomato Tulip	42
White Radish Flower (daikon or mooli)	44
Curly Tops	49
Butter Balls	73
Butter Curls	74

INDEX

Page numbers in *italics* refer to the site of relevant captions.